THE
SHADE

James Robinson

Writer

Cully Hamner Javier Pulido Frazer Irving
Darwyn Cooke J. Bone Jill Thompson Gene Ha

Artists

Dave McCaig Hilary Sycamore Frazer Irving
Dave Stewart Trish Mulvihill Art Lyon

Colorists

Todd Klein

Letterer

Tony Harris

Collection cover artist

Wil Moss *Editor – Original Series*
Rowena Yow *Editor*
Robbin Brosterman *Design Director – Books*

Bob Harras *VP – Editor-in-Chief*

Diane Nelson *President*
Dan DiDio *and* ***Jim Lee*** *Co-Publishers*
Geoff Johns *Chief Creative Officer*
John Rood *Executive VP – Sales, Marketing and Business Development*
Amy Genkins *Senior VP – Business and Legal Affairs*
Nairi Gardiner *Senior VP – Finance*
Jeff Boison *VP – Publishing Operations*
Mark Chiarello *VP – Art Direction and Design*
John Cunningham *VP – Marketing*
Terri Cunningham *VP – Talent Relations and Services*
Alison Gill *Senior VP – Manufacturing and Operations*
Hank Kanalz *Senior VP – Digital*
Jay Kogan *VP – Business and Legal Affairs, Publishing*
Jack Mahan *VP – Business Affairs, Talent*
Nick Napolitano *VP – Manufacturing Administration*
Sue Pohja *VP – Book Sales*
Courtney Simmons *Senior VP – Publicity*
Bob Wayne *Senior VP – Sales*

THE SHADE

DC Comics, 1700 Broadway, New York, NY 10019
A Warner Bros. Entertainment Company
Printed by RR Donnelley, Salem, VA, USA. 1/25/13. First Printing.
ISBN: 978-1-4012-3782-0

Library of Congress Cataloging-in-Publication Data

Robinson, James Dale, author.
The Shade / James Robinson, Cully Hamner, Frazer Irving, Javier Pulido, Gene Ha, Darwyn Cooke, Jill Thompson.
pages cm
"Originally published in single magazine form in The Shade 1-12."
ISBN 978-1-4012-3782-0
1. Graphic novels. I. Hamner, Cully, illustrator. II. Irving, Frazer, illustrator. III. Pulido, Javier, illustrator. IV. Ha, Gene, illustrator. V. Cooke, Darwyn, illustrator. VI. Thompson, Jill, 1966- illustrator. VII. Title.
PN6727.R58S53 2013
741.5'973—dc23
2012046875

Certified Chain of Custody
At Least 20% Certified Forest Content
www.sfiprogram.org
SFI-01042
APPLIES TO TEXT STOCK ONLY

The Shade #1 variant cover art by Cully Hamner

OCTOBER
BRINGS
MELANCHOLY.

OPAL CITY.
EACH YEAR, EVERY YEAR, I FEEL THE SAME. LADEN AND SLUGGISH. NO APPETITE.
WELL, THAT'S NOT GOOD. ANY IDEA WHY?
IT COULD SIMPLY BE SUMMER'S EBB. BUT NO, I'D BE LYING IF I SAID I THOUGHT ***THAT*** WAS THE CAUSE. I KNOW WHY. I ALWAYS HAVE.
THIS IS THE MONTH OF MY CREATION.
MORE TEA?

BY THE WAY, MIKAAL, YOU RECLAIMING THE MANTLE OF STARMAN AGAIN. OPAL. OPAL'S HERO. HAVE I TOLD YOU HOW GLAD...AND PROUD OF YOU I AM?
YOU REALLY SHOULD HAVE DONE IT SOONER, YOU KNOW THAT?

YES, WELL-- YOU'RE RIGHT, OF COURSE. BUT I WAS HAPPY. I WAS IN LOVE. NOW TONY'S DEAD. WHAT ELSE IS THERE FOR ME?
TRAGEDY, IT SEEMS, IS THE GLOOMY, TATTERED THING ALL US METAS ARE DESTINED TO DRAPE AROUND OUR SHOULDERS.

MY, YOU'RE A DELIGHT. TELL ME, DO YOU DROP THESE LITTLE BON MOTS ON YOUR GORILLA FRIEND, TOO? HE MUST LOVE THAT. SUCH DRAMA. "GLOOMY, TATTERED THING" INDEED.
HEAVENS, AND I THOUGHT I WAS IN A FUNK.
STILL, I PRAY THAT WHAT YOU SAY ISN'T TRUE. I'M IN LOVE, YOU SEE.
THE O'DARE GIRL. HOPE? YES, I KNOW. CONGRATULATIONS.
I HAVE TO SAY, I'M GLAD I DON'T HAVE CHILDREN.
I REPEAT: DELIGHTFUL. YOU'RE CERTAINLY NOT HELPING MY MOOD. WHY DON'T WE SKIP THE TEA ENTIRELY AND WATCH AN INGMAR BERGMAN FILM? THAT SHOULD ROUND THINGS OFF NICELY.
I'M SORRY, SHADE. I DON'T KNOW WHAT'S COME OVER ME.
IT'S PROBABLY MY FAULT. I'M SURE IT WAS MY LINE ABOUT OCTOBER THAT GOT YOU GOING.
DON'T WORRY, I'VE HAD DINNER WITH HANS CHRISTIAN ANDERSEN. IF I COULD SIT THROUGH THAT WITHOUT KILLING MYSELF...
STILL, THOUGH, MY DEAR MIKAAL, DO ENDEAVOR TO PUT A SMILE ON IT.

SO, YOU WERE ABOUT TO TELL ME HOW YOU BECAME "THE SHADE." YOUR "SECRET ORIGIN."
I WAS ABOUT TO DO NO SUCH THING.
I MENTIONED OCTOBER BEING THE MONTH OF MY CREATION, BUT I HAVE NO INTENTION OF REVEALING THE HOWS AND WHYS AND ALL THE HORRIFIC EVENTS OF THAT DAY.
ALL I'LL SAY... AGAIN...IS THAT OCTOBER IS THE MONTH OF MY BIRTH, AND AS SUCH...AS SUCH...I'M NOT AT MY BEST.
DO YOU REALLY THINK IT'S POSSIBLE TO LIVE THE LIFE THAT WE DO AND FIND LASTING LOVE?
DEAR GOD, YOU DON'T STOP, DO YOU?
SORRY, BUT NOW MY MIND'S RACING WITH THIS STUFF.
AND CHILDREN? HOW CAN ANY OF US LIVE WITH THE DANGERS WE FACE AND HAVE CHILDREN? I GUESS ANIMAL MAN MANAGES, BUT HE'S THE ONLY ONE WHO COMES TO MIND.
I'M AWARE OF THE PRODIGIOUS MR. BAKER, BUT DO I CARE ONE JOT? DO I GIVE A FIG? I DO NOT.
CHILDREN.

WHAT DID YOU SAY, SHADE? I DIDN'T QUITE--

THE TEA HAS GONE COLD.

I COULD GIVE IT A WARMING NUDGE WITH MY POWER GEM.

NOT WITH MY BEST BONE CHINA, YOU WON'T.

...BONSOIR, GOOD EVENING.
NICE TO MEET YOU. WISH THE CIRCUMSTANCES WERE BETTER, BUT WE CAN'T HAVE EVERYTHING, SO--
HOLD ON--
THIS IS GOING TO HURT.

SO, WHERE WAS I? OH YES, INTRODUCTIONS.
MY NAME--
SORRY, HOLD ON AGAIN.

MY NAME IS **WILLIAM VON HAMMER,** AND I AM...

A) A MAN CURRENTLY IN GREAT DANGER.

B) A MAN WITH A JOB I INTEND TO DO COME HELL OR HIGH WATER.

C) A PRIVATE DETECTIVE.

D) PROBABLY NOT CHARGING ENOUGH FOR MY SERVICES.

E) GERMAN.

F) ALL OF THE ABOVE.

THING IS...THING THEY DON'T KNOW IS...

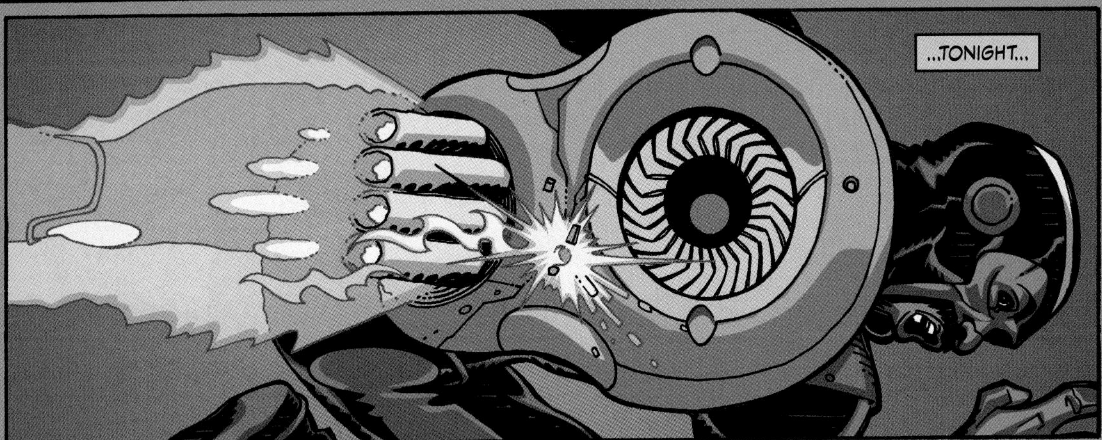
...TONIGHT...

...I'M THE ONLY ONE WHO ISN'T DYING!

NOW. **YOU.** YOUR PARTNERS ARE DEAD. AND YOU ARE NOT FOR **TWO** REASONS.
YOU'RE VERY LUCKY.

HE SHOULD HAVE SPOKEN UP SOONER. FOR HIS OWN SAKE. AS FOR ME...THE HALF WORD HE SAID CONFIRMED WHAT I ALREADY KNEW.

I HAVE TO WARN THE SHADE.

AH, MY DARLING HOPE. POLICE BADGE. PRETTY FACE. HOPE O'DARE. MY LOVE.
I TIDIED UP.

I SEE. YOUR FLAT IS BOTH A BASTION AND A SHRINE TO ORDER.
THOUGH KNOWING ME, PROBABLY ONLY FOR THE NEXT FIVE MINUTES.

HOPE. YOU AND I ARE DIFFERENT.

DUH. YOU THINK?
I THINK IT'S THIS DIFFERENCE THAT...I THINK THAT...

...IF WE ACCEPT IT, DARE I SAY EMBRACE IT, OUR ROMANCE HAS THE BEST CHANCE OF LIFE.
MAN, DICKIE, WILL YOU QUIT WITH ALL THE LOVEY-LOVE-LOVE? WILL WE STAY TOGETHER OR NOT? WHO KNOWS? ENJOY WHAT WE HAVE.

YOU'RE SO BUSY BROODING ABOUT "THE BREAKUP"--WHICH, I MIGHT ADD, HASN'T HAPPENED--THAT YOU'VE STOPPED HAVING FUN.

IN FACT, I HAVE TO SAY...
...YOU'VE STOPPED **BEING** FUN.
WHERE'S THAT RASCAL WITH THE TWINKLING EYE I FELL IN LOVE WITH?

IT'S OCTOBER. NOW. I'M NOT-- I'M...
LOOK, ALL I'M SAYING IS, DON'T GO CHANGING TO TRY TO PLEASE ME.

NUH-UH. THE GREAT DARK SHADE DID NOT JUST QUOTE BILLY JOEL.
BILLY WHO?

LOOK, I APPRECIATE THE SENTIMENT, BUT YOU'RE PUTTING WAY TOO MUCH INTO THIS.
WE LOVE EACH OTHER. ISN'T THAT ENOUGH?
SO YOU ADMIT YOU LOVE ME.

OF COURSE I DO. JEEZUS, I WOULDN'T BE BOTHERING WITH ANY OF THIS IF--LOOK--UM-- THE BOTTOM LINE IS...

...I'M A MESSY TOMBOY WHO LIKES TO SHOOT FELONS AND BITE HER NAILS. YOU'RE...
...NOT.

ALTHOUGH YOU DO DELIGHT IN A CRUELTY TOWARDS YOUR ENEMIES, WHICH IS SOME-THING I CONFESS I'VE ALWAYS FOUND SEXY ABOUT YOU.

YOU NEED TO GET BACK TO BEING THE GUY YOU USED TO BE. AND NOT JUST FOR ME.
FOR YOU, DICKIE.

CRIME? IT'S EXCITING, BUT LIKE OPIUM AND INTERPRETIVE DANCE, ONCE BACK UPON THAT PATH I FEAR IT MIGHT LEAD ME TO RUIN.
NOT CRIME. OF COURSE NOT. I JUST MEANT--

--YOU NEED AN ADVENTURE.

I HAVE TO GO. I'M ON SWINGS FOR THE NEXT TWO WEEKS.
AND I NEED A WALK.

YOU DON'T WALK, DICKIE. YOU AMBLE. YOU STROLL. YOU PROMENADE. YOU TAKE THE AIR.
DON'T TRY TO CHANGE FOR ME EITHER.

I'LL THINK ABOUT YOUR NOTION, BY THE BY.
AN ADVENTURE.

JUST NOTHING THAT TAKES YOU TOO FAR FROM ME, OKAY?

AH, **OPAL CITY!** IT HAS ME. IT HOLDS ME IN ITS SWAY.

HAS. WILL. ALWAYS.

AS DUSK COMES...THE PIGEON-GRAY SKY AND THE SUN'S DEMISE...ITS FINAL DEFIANT HUES OF AMBER AND VERMILLION...

FRAMING THE CITY...

OH, HOW I WISH J. M. W. TURNER WERE ALIVE STILL SO HE MIGHT CAPTURE THIS WONDER.

...OR PERHAPS SOMETHING WILL PRESENT ITSELF.
DEATHSTROKE.
SHADE.

IS THIS A SOCIAL CALL?
NO, STUPID THING TO SAY, EVEN LY. YOU ARE NO MAN FOR SOCIAL.

RECRUITMENT THEN? SOME ERRANT VENTURE REQUIRING MY CIMMERIAN TALENTS?
FLATTERING, BUT BEFORE YOU TELL ME MORE THAN I SHOULD KNOW--
--AND THEREBY FORCE ME TO ACT ACCORDING TO A NEWLY RE-COMPASSED CONSCIENCE--

--I MUST DECLINE.

GOD, YOU LIKE TO TALK.
THIS... ME HERE...IT'S BUSINESS.

AH, YOU SEEK MY DEATH.

WELL, GOOD LUCK WITH THAT.
DON'T BELIEVE IN LUCK.

AH... AH...
ROBOT! COURTESY OF SOME FRIENDS IN HIGH PLACES...

THIS--
--COURTESY OF ME!
I KNOW...
NOTHING PERSONAL.

...I KNOW I'VE SAID THIS AND THOUGHT THIS AND FELT THIS SO MANY TIMES BEFORE...
...BUT PERHAPS IN THIS INSTANCE, THE REMARK BEARS REPEATING...

OCTOBER BRINGS MELANCHOLY.
BIRTHDAY
JAMES ROBINSON writer
CULLY HAMNER artist
DAVE McCAIG colors
TODD KLEIN letters
TONY HARRIS cover artist

HARRIS

The Shade #2 variant cover art by Cully Hamner

"THE ARROGANCE OF DEATHSTROKE.
"UNMITIGATED GALL.

"I HAVE BEEN IMMORTAL SINCE 1838. I HAVE FOUGHT DEMONS AND JEALOUS HUSBANDS, BRIDGE TROLLS AND RAZOR-WIELDING ICE CREAM VENDORS.

"STEAM-DRIVEN ROBOTS, PHANTOM EXECUTIONERS, ANGELS, DRAGONS AND DIVAS.

"NOT TO MENTION MY DUEL OF ACID AND SHADOW WITH THE 'SCOURGE OF THE ORIENT,' DR. LEI-SU YUNG.

"PFFT.
"A ONE-EYED ASSASSIN, WEIGHED DOWN BY CHAIN MAIL AND PRIDE, IS BUT A STROLL IN SPRING WHEN I CATALOGUE MY JOURNEY TO DATE.

"OF COURSE, DEATHSTROKE IS A FORMIDABLE CHAP.
"BUT I'VE FACED WORSE.
"TRUTHFULLY, I SENSED HIS PRESENCE MINUTES BEFORE HE MADE HIMSELF KNOWN.
"IN THE TREES, IN THE PARK, I STEPPED INTO SHADOW...AND A FACSIMILE OF MYSELF STEPPED OUT, SPEAKING WITH MY UBIQUITOUS APLOMB, BUT MADE OF NOTHING BUT THE DARKNESS THAT BRED IT.
"IT WILL FADE BACK TO NOTHING SOON.
THOSE FIRST FEW STEPS
JAMES ROBINSON writer
CULLY HAMNER artist
DAVE McCAIG colorist
TODD KLEIN letterer
TONY HARRIS cover artist
"AND I WILL NOT."

I UNDERSTOOD, LIKE, MAYBE EVERY OTHER WORD OF THAT LAST PART, BUT GO ON.

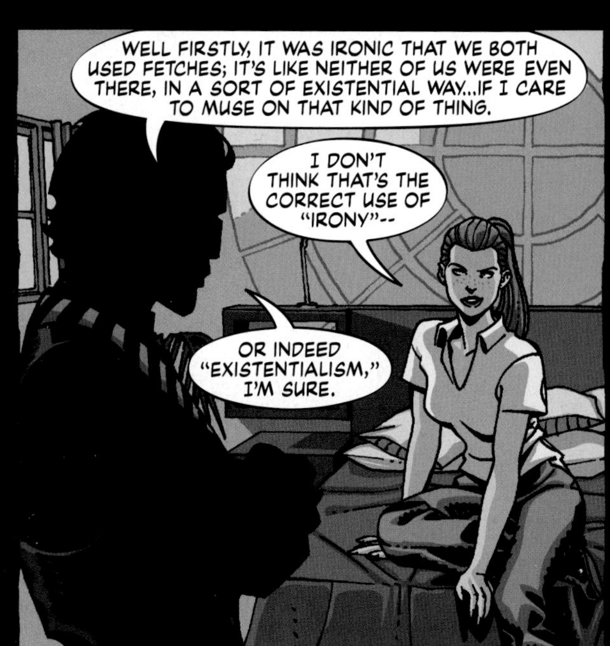
WELL FIRSTLY, IT WAS IRONIC THAT WE BOTH USED FETCHES; IT'S LIKE NEITHER OF US WERE EVEN THERE, IN A SORT OF EXISTENTIAL WAY...IF I CARE TO MUSE ON THAT KIND OF THING.
I DON'T THINK THAT'S THE CORRECT USE OF "IRONY"--
OR INDEED "EXISTENTIALISM," I'M SURE.

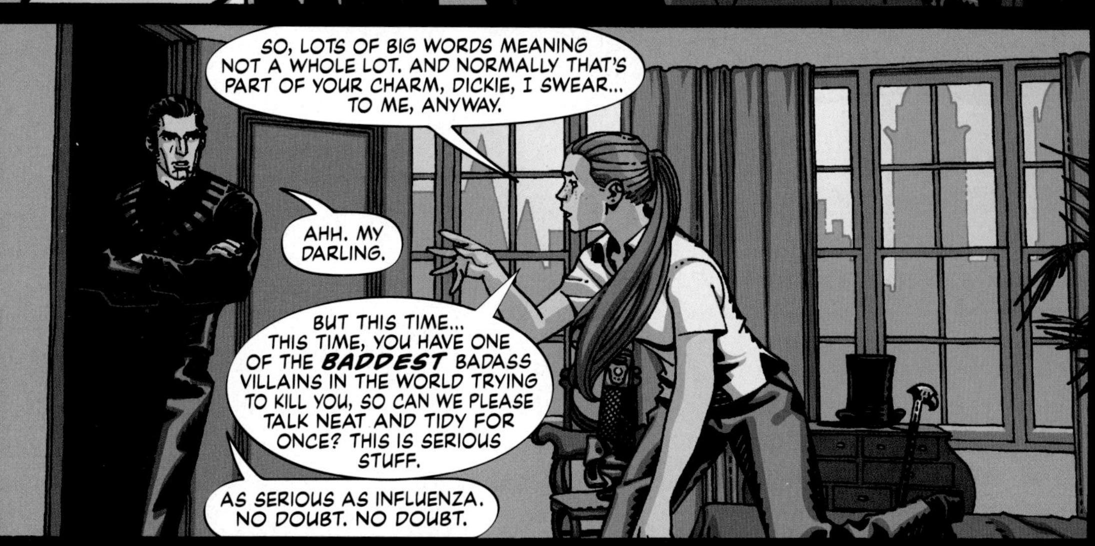
SO, LOTS OF BIG WORDS MEANING NOT A WHOLE LOT. AND NORMALLY THAT'S PART OF YOUR CHARM, DICKIE, I SWEAR... TO ME, ANYWAY.
AHH. MY DARLING.
BUT THIS TIME... THIS TIME, YOU HAVE ONE OF THE BADDEST BADASS VILLAINS IN THE WORLD TRYING TO KILL YOU, SO CAN WE PLEASE TALK NEAT AND TIDY FOR ONCE? THIS IS SERIOUS STUFF.
AS SERIOUS AS INFLUENZA. NO DOUBT. NO DOUBT.

WHICH IS WHY I'M HERE AT YOUR APARTMENT AND NOT AT MY OWN ABODE. THIS FOLLOWING ON FROM WHY I FAKED MY DEATH IN THE FIRST PLACE.
I COULD HAVE KILLED DEATHSTROKE. BUT THAT'S ALL I WOULD HAVE DONE.
IF I'D TORTURED HIM TO LEARN WHO HIRED HIM, HE WOULDN'T HAVE TOLD ME. NOT SLADE WILSON.

BUT AS DANGEROUS AS HE IS, IN THE END WILSON IS JUST THE AGENT FOR SOMEONE ELSE'S INTENTIONS.

SOMEONE WANTS ME DEAD. I MEAN TO DISCOVER ***WHO.***
THE LUDLOWS?
THE LAST SURVIVOR, WHOSE LIFE I IN FACT SPARED ONCE UPON A TIME, SUCCUMBED TO PANCREATIC CANCER LAST YEAR, I'M SORRY TO SAY. SO NO, NOT THE LUDLOWS.

IT'S ***BETTER*** THE WORLD THINKS ME DEAD. I CAN TRAVEL THAT WORLD ALL THE EASIER UNHINDERED AND UNNOTICED.
WELL, GOOD LUCK GOING UNNOTICED, DICKIE, BUT I GET YOUR POINT.
BUT I COULDN'T BEAR TO GO WITHOUT A FAREWELL. NOR COULD I BEAR TO THINK YOU MIGHT HEAR OF MY DEATH AND BELIEVE IT SO.
OH, YOU THINK I'D BE ALL BROKEN UP, HUH?

OKAY, I'D BE DEVASTATED.

I'LL BE BACK, HOPE. WHEN IT'S SAFE TO WALK THE STREETS OF MY CITY AGAIN. YOU UNDERSTAND, I TRUST...IT'S NOT FOR MYSELF THAT I FEAR, BUT THOSE I CARE ABOUT WHO I MIGHT BE SO LUCKY AS TO TAKE THOSE WALKS WITH.
DICKIE--
NO. I'M SORRY, I CALL YOU THAT 'CAUSE IT'S FUNNY, BUT WHAT I HAVE TO SAY NOW ISN'T. IT'S NOT SOMETHING I SAY LIGHTLY... IT'S SOMETHING I'M SCARED TO SAY, ACTUALLY. BUT HERE GOES:
RICHARD...
...I LOVE YOU.

SO...

...WHERE WERE WE LAST TIME?

PERSÖNLICH
UNTERSUCHUNG
VÖLLIG LIZENSIERT

ROOFTOP CHASE WITH LES DIABOLIQUES. THEY DIED, I DIDN'T.

THAT'S RIGHT, IT'S ***ALL*** COMING BACK TO ME.

SO WHERE WERE WE? SEE, FORGETTING AGAIN.
I'VE GOTTEN WORD OFF THAT I HOPE WILL GET TO THE SHADE ABOUT THE THINGS THAT I'VE UNCOVERED.
PEOPLE WHO DON'T WANT THOSE TIDBITS COMING TO LIGHT HAVE SENT OTHERS TO KILL ME AFTER LES DIABOLIQUES DIDN'T PROVE UP TO THE TASK.
LES DIABOLIQUES WERE BELGIAN. THESE NEW ONES ARE FRENCH. SOUTH. MARSEILLE. ROUGH BUNCH...
...BUT HONESTLY, THEY'RE NO TROUBLE...THUGS, SOME OF THEM TOUGH, SURE. TOUGH. BUT NO MORE DANGEROUS THAN LES DIABOLIQUES.
MY CURRENT PLAYMATE BEING A PRIME EXAMPLE.
NO...
...IT'S THEIR BOSS THAT WORRIES ME.
WORD IS HE'S TAKING MY CONTINUED EXISTENCE PERSONALLY... THAT HE'S COMING TO GET ME HIMSELF.

AND HE PLAYS A LITTLE ROUGHER.
OH, AND FOR ALL OF YOU VISITING HAMBURG, GERMANY, FOR THE FIRST TIME, I'M SORRY...SHOULD HAVE INTRODUCED MYSELF.
I'M WILL VON HAMMER, PRIVATE DETECTIVE AND A SEX MACHINE WITH ALL THE CHICKS.
(ACTUALLY I'M NOT, BUT I'VE ALWAYS WANTED TO SAY THAT.)

AVIARY SUPPER CLUB.
OF OPAL. A FITTING PLACE, I
POSE, FOR MY **FINAL** MEETING...
...ONE FINAL PERSON TO SEE BEFORE I GO.
JAKE BENNETTI, BETTER KNOWN BY HIS SOBRIQUET...
BOBO. A PLEASURE AS ALWAYS.
AND **ALWAYS** A PLEASURE BACK, BUDDY. GOTTA SAY, THOUGH, NOT THE BEST TIME FOR A MEET 'N' GREET. NOT FOR YOURS TRULY...
THERE'S A CERTAIN CUTE BIG-BREASTED WIDOW ACROSS TOWN WHOSE SHEETS ARE ICY, ME BEING HERE, JUST SO YOU KNOW.
LET'S BE QUICK THEN, WHICH IS FINE BY ME--THIS PLACE IS HARDLY "INCOGNITO."
I HAVE TO GO AWAY...DON'T ASK ME WHY, BECAUSE I

I WANTED TO SEE YOU... TO ASK YOU...TO TAKE EXTRA CARE OF OPAL FOR ME. PLEASE. AND PLEASE, *PLEASE* KEEP A WATCHFUL EYE ON HOPE...
...BUT FOR GOD'S SAKE, DON'T LET HER KNOW--SHE'LL KILL ME.
AND ME, BROTHER. AND ME. I'LL BE OH SO ON THE DOWN BELOW.
AND YOU'RE ABOUT TO 23 SKIDOO...DON'T SUPPOSE IT'S GOT ANYTHING TO DO WITH THE BRIGHT RED TARGET ON THAT NICE BLACK SUIT OF YOURS?
AND *HOW,* PRAY TELL, WOULD YOU KNOW ABOUT THAT?
FUNNY THING... COINCIDENCE. COME MORNING I WAS GOING TO SEE YOU ANYWAY ON ACCOUNT'A I GOT A MESSAGE. HOUR AGO, MAYBE. HOUR AND CHANGE.
CAT I CROSSED PATHS WITH DURING A CRAZY CAPER IN MOROCCO A FEW YEARS BACK. VAMPIRE GIGOLO HIT MEN...DON'T ASK.
ANYWAY, THIS GUY CALLS ME, TRANS-AT, NO LESS...HAMBURG, GERMANY.
HE WANTS YOU TO KNOW THAT SOMEONE WANTS YOU *DEAD.* SAYS HE KNOWS *MORE,* BUT YOU HAVE TO GO SEE HIM.
SAYS THERE'S A NAME YOU'LL KNOW...INVOLVED IN ALL THIS.
NAME?
CALDECOTT.

WHERE DO HOTELS FIND THEIR SHEETS AND FURNITURE AND ART FOR THE WALLS? WHAT OASIS OF "SAME" DO THEY ALL RIDE THEIR CAMELS UP TO?

I THINK SUCH THOUGHTS AS I CLEAN MY GUN AND LISTEN TO ZERO 7.

AND LIKE THEIR LYRICS, I HAVE "GONE TO GROUND." I MIGHT ***INDEED*** HAVE BEEN "WATCHING PORN" IN A "DRESSING GOWN" TOO IF THE HOTELS DIDN'T CHARGE SO MUCH FOR ADULT FILMS. AND THE FACT IS, I MAY GET ATTACKED AT ANY MOMENT, SO DRESSING GOWNS ARE OUT OF THE QUESTION.

YES, I'M HIDING OUT.

THE FRENCH MOB BOSS I SPOKE OF HAS ARRIVED IN TOWN, AND THE HUNT FOR ME IS ON, SO I'M--

BONJOUR. VON HAMMER, *NON?* YES? NO?

...BUT I HAVE TO SAY, BETE-NOIRE, YOU ARE A BORE AND A BULLY.

I'VE KILLED PEOPLE FOR BEING ONE OR THE OTHER IN THE PAST, DID YOU KNOW THAT?

IMAGINE WHAT I'M GOING TO DO TO YOU.

I'VE BEEN WAITING FOR THIS! THE MIGHTY SHADE! SO "POWERFUL"! SO "SHADOW-STRONG"! WE WILL SEE!
ENGLISH! I HATE ON YOU!
YES, FRENCH MAN, AND SOAP, TOO, ACCORDING TO PUBLIC CONSENSUS.
IT'S REASSURING...HOW SOME XENOPHOBIC DISDAINS APPARENTLY NEVER DIE.
ME...

MY WORLD...

..AND THAT OF THE SHADE, TOO, I'M GUESSING...

DEBATE AND COMPROMISE?

SCANT WIGGLE ROOM.

AND...

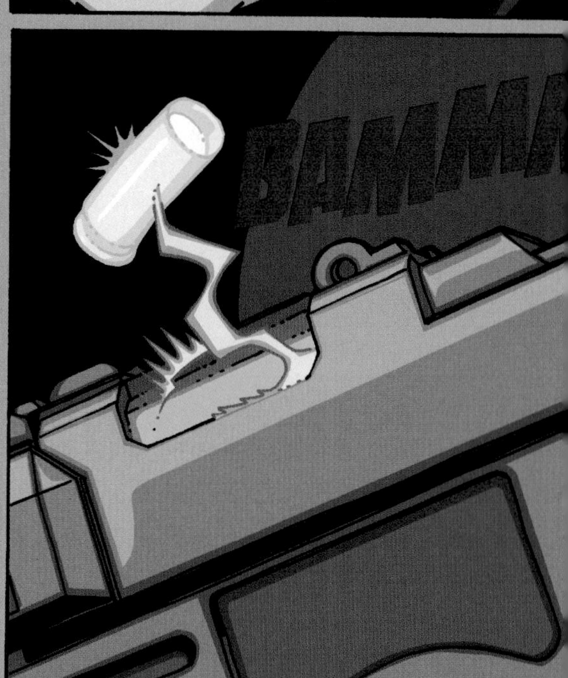
BAMM

...DONE.
IT SEEMS YOU ARE, TOO.
WELL, I APPEAR TO HAVE KILLED EVERYONE I CAN, SO YES.

THEN BY ALL MEANS, VON HAMMER, LET US AWAY.

HERE!
WE CAN SEE ANY FURTHER ATTACKERS COMING FROM ALL SIDES... THOUGH I DOUBT THEY'D THINK TO LOOK HERE.
SO YOU DID IT?
"IT"?
KILLED BETE-NOIRE. HELL OF A THING. HONESTLY, I DIDN'T KNOW YOU SHADOW TYPES COULD DIE.
I DIDN'T. WE CAN'T--DIE, THAT IS. NO...
...I EVOKED A...SPELL, I SUPPOSE YOU'D CALL IT...DESTABILIZED HIS SHADOW-MATTER AND ABSORBED IT BACK INTO THE VOID.
IT WILL TAKE HIM MONTHS TO RECONSTITUTE HIMSELF, AND BY THEN, HOPEFULLY, WE'LL BE DONE WITH ALL THIS, YOU AND I, ASSUMING YOU TELL ME...
...WHAT IN GOD'S NAME ALL THIS IS. SIMPLY TOLD, NOW.
WELL, I KNOW OF YOU...HEARD ABOUT YOU FROM JAKE BENNETTI DURING AN EXPLOIT--
YES, GIGOLO HIT MEN...VAMPIRES, NO LESS...YES, YES, DO GET TO IT.

BOY, YOU ARE NOT THE FUN-LOVING FELLOW I IMAGINED.
OH, I'M CHUCKLES A-PLENTY. BUT NOT TONIGHT--I FEAR A MIGRAINE. COME. SPEAK. SCHNELL.
VERY WELL...

I WAS HIRED TO FIND OUT IF THERE WERE ANY SAMPLES OF YOUR BLOOD STILL IN EXISTENCE.

MY BLOOD?
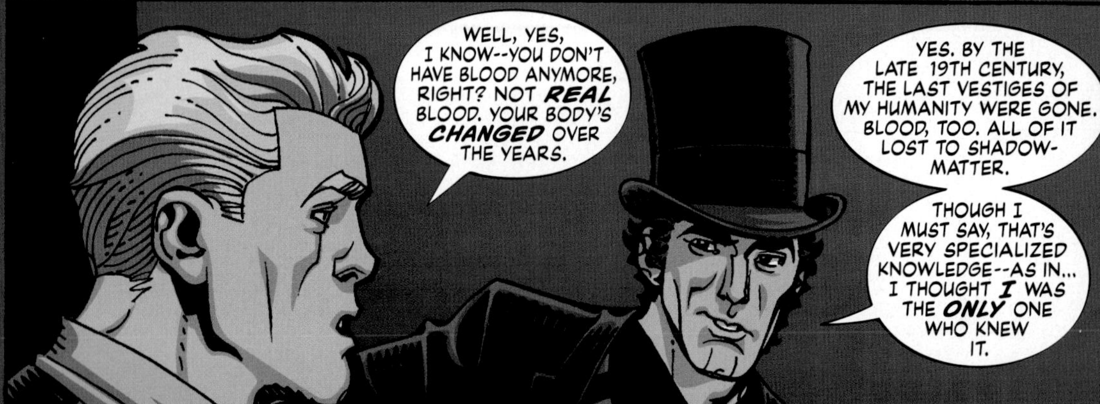
WELL, YES, I KNOW--YOU DON'T HAVE BLOOD ANYMORE, RIGHT? NOT REAL BLOOD. YOUR BODY'S CHANGED OVER THE YEARS.
YES. BY THE LATE 19TH CENTURY, THE LAST VESTIGES OF MY HUMANITY WERE GONE. BLOOD, TOO. ALL OF IT LOST TO SHADOW-MATTER.
THOUGH I MUST SAY, THAT'S VERY SPECIALIZED KNOWLEDGE--AS IN... I THOUGHT I WAS THE ONLY ONE WHO KNEW IT.

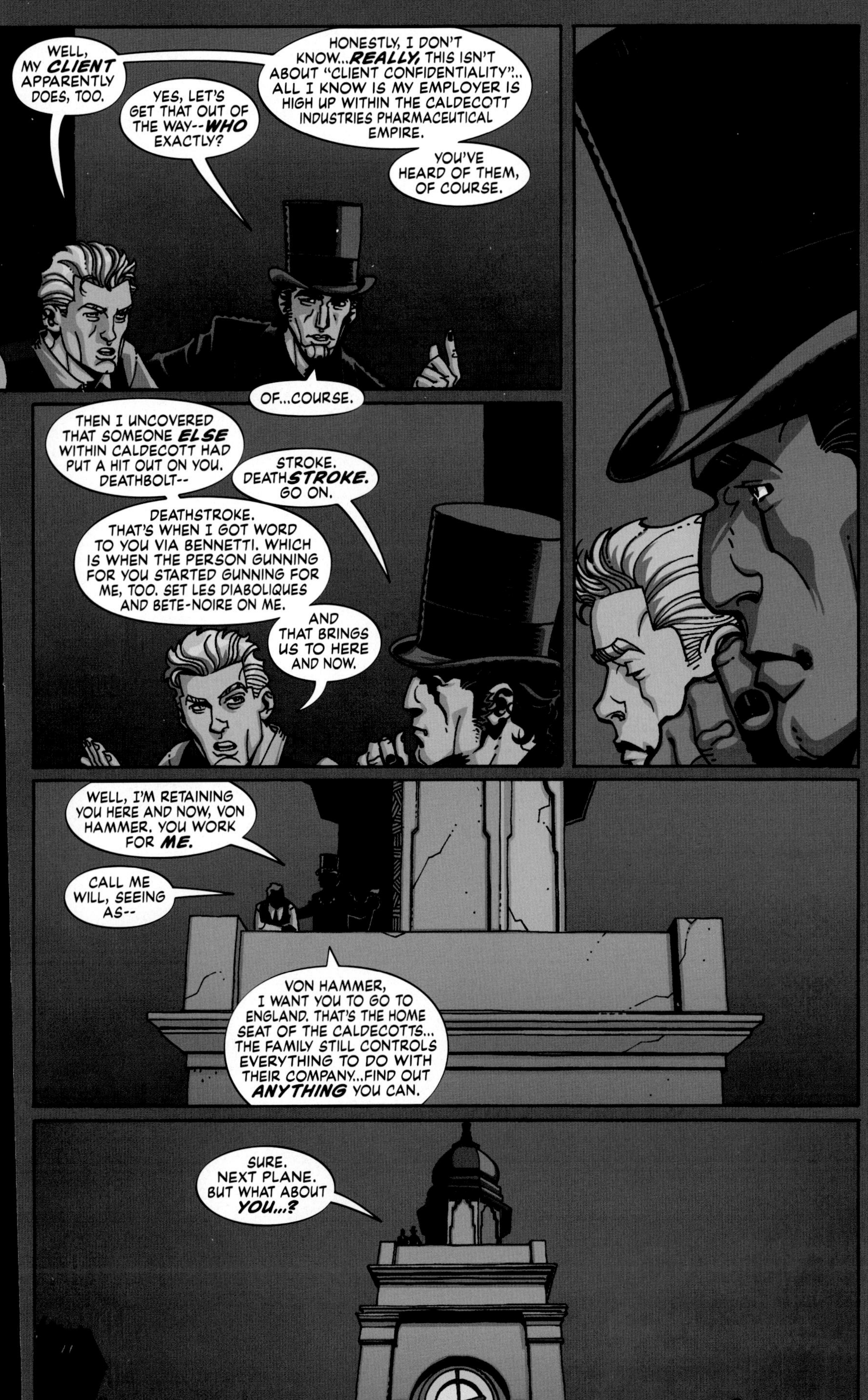
WELL, MY CLIENT APPARENTLY DOES, TOO.
YES, LET'S GET THAT OUT OF THE WAY--WHO EXACTLY?
HONESTLY, I DON'T KNOW...REALLY, THIS ISN'T ABOUT "CLIENT CONFIDENTIALITY"... ALL I KNOW IS MY EMPLOYER IS HIGH UP WITHIN THE CALDECOTT INDUSTRIES PHARMACEUTICAL EMPIRE.
YOU'VE HEARD OF THEM, OF COURSE.
OF...COURSE.
THEN I UNCOVERED THAT SOMEONE ELSE WITHIN CALDECOTT HAD PUT A HIT OUT ON YOU. DEATHBOLT--
STROKE. DEATHSTROKE. GO ON.
DEATHSTROKE. THAT'S WHEN I GOT WORD TO YOU VIA BENNETTI. WHICH IS WHEN THE PERSON GUNNING FOR YOU STARTED GUNNING FOR ME, TOO. SET LES DIABOLIQUES AND BETE-NOIRE ON ME.
AND THAT BRINGS US TO HERE AND NOW.
WELL, I'M RETAINING YOU HERE AND NOW, VON HAMMER. YOU WORK FOR ME.
CALL ME WILL, SEEING AS--
VON HAMMER, I WANT YOU TO GO TO ENGLAND. THAT'S THE HOME SEAT OF THE CALDECOTTS... THE FAMILY STILL CONTROLS EVERYTHING TO DO WITH THEIR COMPANY...FIND OUT ANYTHING YOU CAN.
SURE. NEXT PLANE. BUT WHAT ABOUT YOU...?

"...WHERE ARE *YOU* GOING?"
AUSTRALIA.
HE'LL BE HERE SOON, I SENSE IT.
UNAVOIDABLE. *INEVITABLE.*
I WILL BE *READY!*

The Shade #3 variant cover art by Cully Hamner

THE SCHOONER CRESTED OVER A PARTICULARLY LARGE WAVE...

...AND COMING DOWN, THE WATERS PARTED LIKE CURTAINS ON A STAGE, REVEALING, UNVEILING, PRESENTING BOTANY BAY.

THIS WAS 1874, OF COURSE. BEFORE I'D MASTERED MY ABILITY TO "STEP" THROUGH THE SHADOWS FROM ONE LOCATION TO ANOTHER, HENCE THE ARDUOUS, MIRTHLESS MANNER OF MY ARRIVAL.

I HAD TAKEN A JOB--

NO, NOT A "JOB." THAT MAKES ME SOUND LIKE A PLUMBER OR A SWEEP. THIS WAS AN **ASSIGNMENT.** A MISSING HEIR, AND THE PROMISE OF ONE TENTH OF HIS FORTUNE IF I RECOVERED HIM. A TALE OF BUNYIPS AND BAD MEN...FOR ANOTHER TIME.

...COMPARED TO TODAY.
THIS IMPROBABLE SCENE IS THANKS TO CHIEF INSPECTOR PEMULWUY OF THE NEW SOUTH WALES POLICE, OF WHOM I REQUIRE INFORMATION AND GUIDANCE.
HE, IN RETURN, BIDS ME AID A LOCAL HERO AGAINST THE UNSAVORY ACTIONS OF THE IDLE HANDS, A GROUP WHOSE SAID AFFRONT THIS DAY INCLUDES THEM PROFITING IN SOME MANNER FROM THE DESTRUCTION OF THE SYDNEY OPERA HOUSE.
AS FOR THE HERO THAT I ASSIST...

DREAMTIME

...THE ARGONAUT...
...I ASSUME HE IS PART OF THE VAST GREEK COMMUNITY IN THE CITY. (OTHERWISE HIS MONIKER MAKES NO SENSE AT ALL.)
I COULD ASK HIM, OF COURSE, BUT HE DOESN'T SEEM TOO CHATTY.
JAMES ROBINSON writer
CULLY HAMNER artist
DAVE McCAIG colorist
TODD KLEIN letterer
TONY HARRIS cover artist

SO, YOUR MESS IS SWEPT.
HMMPT

I GUESS. HERE THEN, MY PART OF THE DEAL.
DARNELL CALDECOTT TOOK THE ALIAS OF JOHN CROSS. HE LIVES IN A REMOTE...ERR...I DON'T KNOW WHAT YOU'D CALL IT...VILLA? FORTRESS? HUGE PLACE ON A TABLE MOUNTAIN JUST OUTSIDE OF ALICE.
THANK YOU, PEMULWUY.

ALICE?
SPRINGS. ALICE SPRINGS. PRETTY MUCH THE CENTER OF THE COUNTRY.
SO CALDECOTT'S GONE THE WAY OF THE HERMETIC, LOOPY BILLIONAIRE LIVING IN SECLUSION?
IT'D SEEM SO.

GUARDS, I SUPPOSE. LOTS.
YOU'D SUPPOSE THAT, WOULDN'T YOU? I CERTAINLY DID. 'S NOT IT, THOUGH, NOT "LOTS" OF GUARDS--JUST THE ONE, IN FACT.

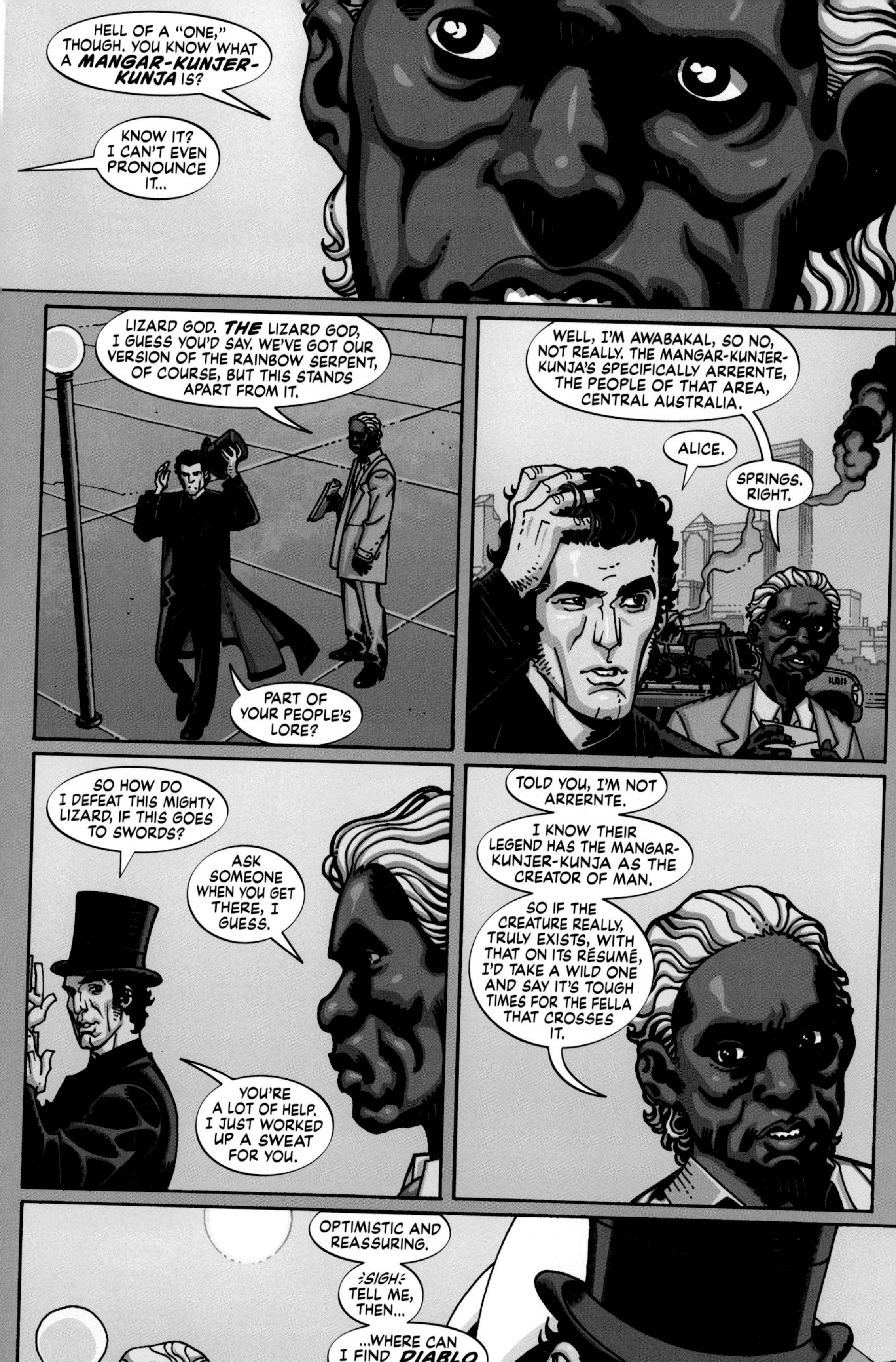

HELL OF A "ONE," THOUGH. YOU KNOW WHAT A MANGAR-KUNJER-KUNJA IS?
KNOW IT? I CAN'T EVEN PRONOUNCE IT...
LIZARD GOD. THE LIZARD GOD, I GUESS YOU'D SAY. WE'VE GOT OUR VERSION OF THE RAINBOW SERPENT, OF COURSE, BUT THIS STANDS APART FROM IT.
PART OF YOUR PEOPLE'S LORE?
WELL, I'M AWABAKAL, SO NO, NOT REALLY. THE MANGAR-KUNJER-KUNJA'S SPECIFICALLY ARRERNTE, THE PEOPLE OF THAT AREA, CENTRAL AUSTRALIA.
ALICE.
SPRINGS. RIGHT.
SO HOW DO I DEFEAT THIS MIGHTY LIZARD, IF THIS GOES TO SWORDS?
ASK SOMEONE WHEN YOU GET THERE, I GUESS.
YOU'RE A LOT OF HELP. I JUST WORKED UP A SWEAT FOR YOU.
TOLD YOU, I'M NOT ARRERNTE.
I KNOW THEIR LEGEND HAS THE MANGAR-KUNJER-KUNJA AS THE CREATOR OF MAN.
SO IF THE CREATURE REALLY, TRULY EXISTS, WITH THAT ON ITS RÉSUMÉ, I'D TAKE A WILD ONE AND SAY IT'S TOUGH TIMES FOR THE FELLA THAT CROSSES IT.
OPTIMISTIC AND REASSURING.
SIGH TELL ME, THEN...
...WHERE CAN I FIND DIABLO BLACKSMITH?

I SUPPOSE I SHOULD ELUCIDATE THAT THE SECOND TIME I VISITED AUSTRALIA MANY YEARS AGO, MY INTENTIONS WERE FAR LESS NOBLE.
WAS (HALFHEARTEDLY, I DMIT) PLANNING A ROBBERY. EWELRY. MUSEUM EXHIBIT. LAH, BLAH, SAME OLD, SAME OLD.
ANYWAY, IN THE COURSE OF MY LARK, I CROSSED PATHS WITH A STAGE MAGICIAN CUM CRIME-FIGHTER/SLEUTH, ONE DIABLO BLACKSMITH.
AND NOT IN A FRIENDLY MANNER.
THOUGH HIS MAGICAL ABILITIES MIGHT BE LESS THAN THOSE OF THE COMELY ZATANNA, HE MADE UP FOR THIS WITH A KNOWLEDGE OF MAGICAL LORE AND AN UNERRING DEDUCTIVE EYE.
NEEDLESS TO SAY, WE DID NOT PART AS FRIENDS.
DIABLO BLACKSMITH!
NOW · APPEAR
DIABLO.
SHADE.

PEMULWUY ASSURES ME YOU'RE HERE FOR ADVICE, NOT REVENGE OR ANY KIND OF WRONGDOING.
ABSOLUTELY, MY FRIEND. YOU CAN PUT AWAY THE SPELL-BOOK.
I'M NOT YOUR FRIEND.
UNDERSTOOD. THEN LET US BE ABOUT THIS SO I CAN BE ON MY WAY ALL THE SOONER. I NEED TO KNOW WHAT I'M GETTING INTO...WHAT I'M GOING UP AGAINST. A MANGAR-KUNJER-KUNJA... CREATOR OF THE WORLD?

NO, THAT'S ALCHERA, ACCORDING TO THE ARRERNTE. MANGAR-KUNJER-KUNJA CREATED PEOPLE...
...CUT THE FIRST MEN FROM THE SIDE OF A HILL, CUT HOLES IN THEM FOR THEIR MOUTH, EARS AND NOSES, GAVE THEM WEAPONS AND FIRE.

SO HOW MUCH OF A THREAT IS THIS CREATURE? BREEZE OR BROOK?
IN TERMS OF THE MANGAR-KUNJER-KUNJA'S LEGEND, I'D NOTE HIS ONENESS WITH FIRE AND KNIVES.

CAN'T BE GOOD.

SO HOW DO I DEFEAT THIS CREATURE?
YOU'VE A ONENESS WITH SHADOW--NO ONE MORE SO ON THE PLANET, I'D SAY. THAT'LL HELP, OF COURSE, BUT WHAT YOU REALLY NEED...

...IS ONENESS WITH DREAMTIME.

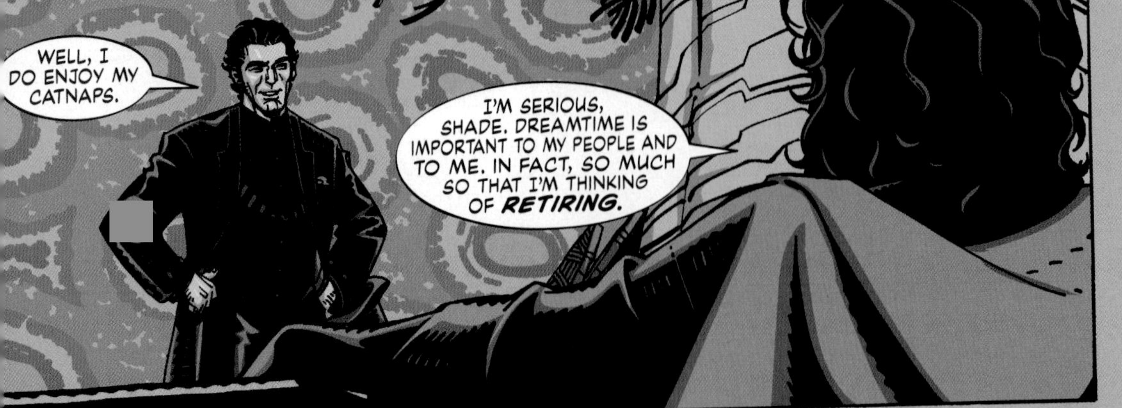
WELL, I DO ENJOY MY CATNAPS.
I'M SERIOUS, SHADE. DREAMTIME IS IMPORTANT TO MY PEOPLE AND TO ME. IN FACT, SO MUCH SO THAT I'M THINKING OF *RETIRING*.

FROM STAGE OR STREET?
PERFORMING IS MY LIFE, I COULD *NEVER* BID IT GOOD-BYE. CRIME FIGHTING, ON THE OTHER HAND...

HONESTLY, I LOVE THE RUSH. THE THRILL OF THE HUNT AND THE ACCLAIM THAT FOLLOWS A VICTORY. I HAVE AN EGO, I ADMIT IT.

BUT IT COSTS ME, YOU SEE. MY OWN ONENESS WITH DREAM-TIME.
OR IN THE WORDS OF YOUR PEOPLE...
...I FEEL I AM LOSING MY SOUL.

I'M BLESSED WITH THE LACK OF ONE, SO NOT A PROBLEM.
THAT'S WHAT YOU LIKE TO SAY...MAYBE YOU EVEN BELIEVE IT, TOO. BUT I SEE YOUR SOUL, SHADE. HERE, NOW, I SEE IT GROWING.
YOUR JOURNEY, THIS CHANGE IN HOW YOU ARE...IT'S *IMPORTANT* THAT YOU KEEP ON THE PATH.

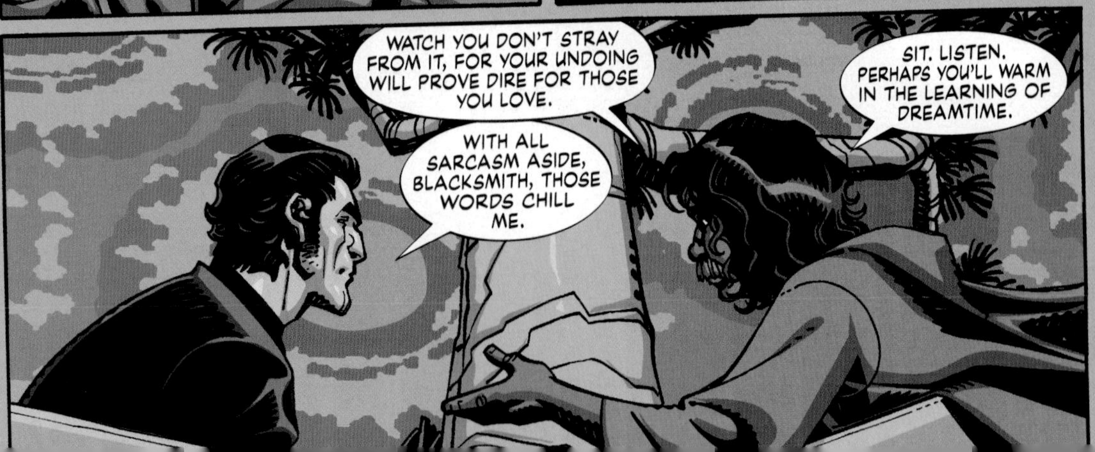
WATCH YOU DON'T STRAY FROM IT, FOR YOUR UNDOING WILL PROVE DIRE FOR THOSE YOU LOVE.
SIT. LISTEN. PERHAPS YOU'LL WARM IN THE LEARNING OF DREAMTIME.
WITH ALL SARCASM ASIDE, BLACKSMITH, THOSE WORDS CHILL ME.

POPULARIZED (SOMEWHAT) BY NEVIL SHUTE IN 1950, ALICE SPRINGS IS THE SECOND BIGGEST TOWN IN THE NORTHERN TERRITORIES.
HOT, DRY, AND ABOVE ALL, DUSTY, I'TS NOT SOMEWHERE I'D PLACE HIGH ON A MENU OF DESTINATIONS--NOTWITHSTANDING ITS ANNUAL CAMEL RACE.
AND DESPITE THAT, THE MIXTURE OF CULTURES... WHITE SETTLER AND ABORIGINE...ARE BOTH IDENTIFIED HERE...
...AND CERTAINLY "ALICE" IS HOME TO MANY ORIGINAL NATIVES.
WELCOME TO
ALICE SPRIN
IT'S ONLY WHEN I GET OUT OF TOWN... INTO THE DESERTS...THAT I BEGIN TO FEEL THE TRUE HISTORY. THE PAST. THE PAST OF THE ARRERNTE PEOPLE WHEN THEY CALLED THIS LAND "MPARNTWE."
THEY BELIEVE THE HILLS AND GORGES AND GRAND DESIGN OF THE EARTH WERE SHAPED BY CREATURES IN ANCIENT TIMES...DINGOES, CATERPILLARS AND WALLAROOS, AMONG OTHERS.
LIZARDS, TOO, FROM WHAT I CAN SEE AT THIS MOMENT IN TIME.
FOR INDEED, YOU MAY BE ENJOYING THE MAJESTIC VIEW OF DARNELL CALDECOTT'S HOME...

...BUT NOT I.

SOME MAGICK IS AT WORK...HAS TO BE. MAKING THIS DELIGHTFUL SPECTACLE OF THE MANGAR-KUNJER-KUNJA INVISIBLE TO ALL BUT MYSELF.
LUCKY FELLOW THAT I AM.
THE CREATURE APPEARS IMMUNE TO MY SHADOW...
...AND HAS AN AVERSION TO ME BASED ON NOTHING I CAN FATHOM.

I WISH I WAS BETTER AT LISTENING. I **REALLY** DO.
ALL THOSE HOURS I SPENT TRYING TO UNDERSTAND WHAT BLACKSMITH WAS GOING ON ABOUT... "DREAMTIME THIS" AND "DREAMING THAT"...
...FACTS THAT HAVE NOW DESERTED ME LIKE THE CALLOW ADMIRERS OF EVELYN NESBIT.
WHY DO YOU DENY ME ENTRY?
I MUST: YOUR EVIL IS TOO GREAT TO RISK MY CHARGE IN ALL HIS WEAKNESS AND WISDOM.
YOUR "CHARGE"? YOU MEAN DARNELL CALDECOTT?
LISTEN TO ME...

...I MEAN HIM NO HARM... NOR YOU, FOR THAT MATTER... ERR...
...DO YOU HAVE A NAME? I MEAN, I KNOW YOU'RE A MANGAR-KUNJER-KUNJA...A LIZARD GOD. HONESTLY DIDN'T EXPECT YOU TO BE SO BIG...BUT THAT'S ME, ALL OVER...
...I MEAN, BY NOW YOU'D THINK I'D EXPECT THE UNEXPECTED, BUT OH NO--
YOUR WORDS...
...MEANINGLESS...
...AND FAILING TO MASK YOUR WANTON, SAD VILLAINY.

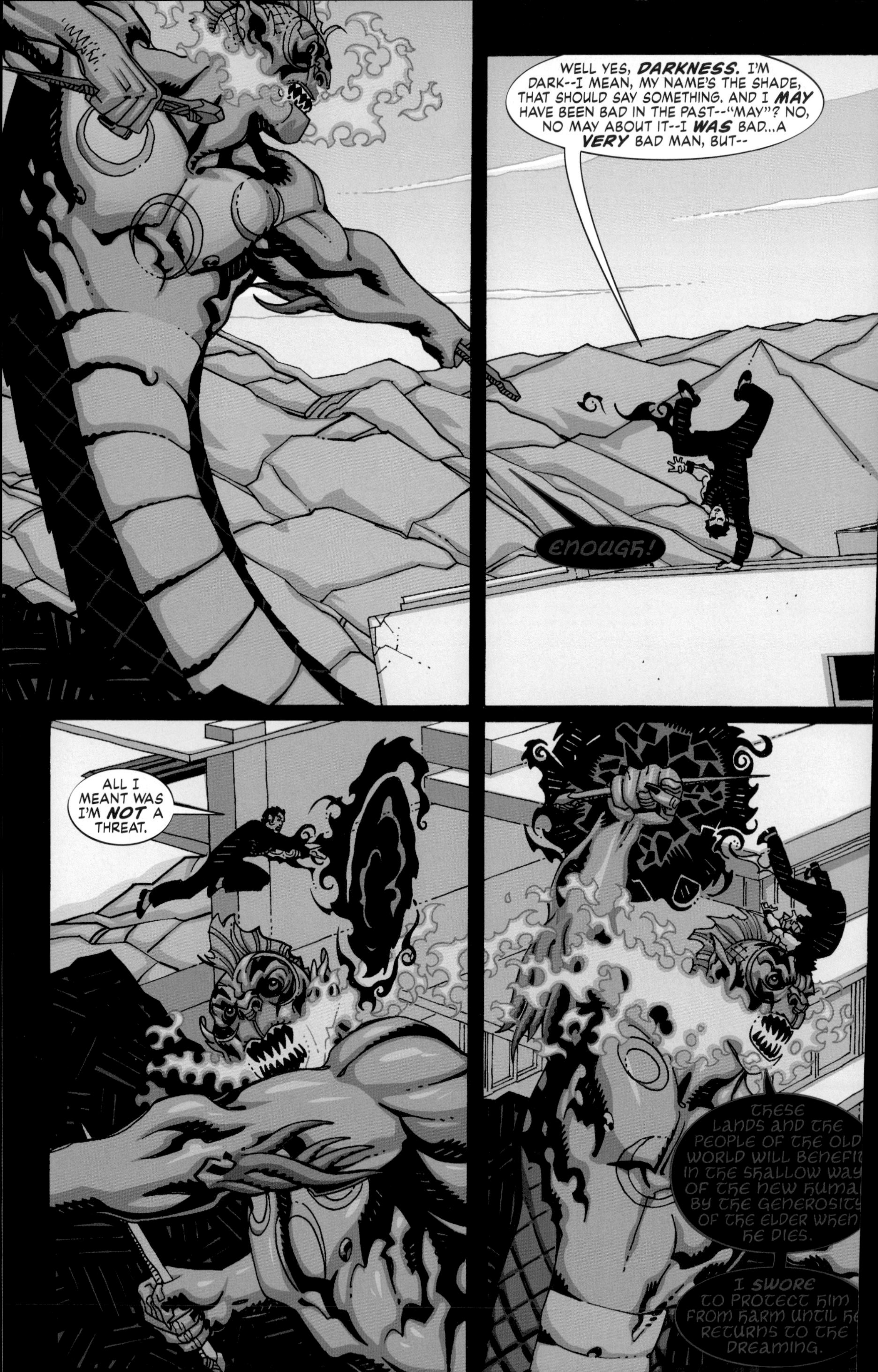

WELL YES, DARKNESS. I'M DARK--I MEAN, MY NAME'S THE SHADE, THAT SHOULD SAY SOMETHING. AND I MAY HAVE BEEN BAD IN THE PAST--"MAY"? NO, NO MAY ABOUT IT--I WAS BAD...A VERY BAD MAN, BUT--
ENOUGH!
ALL I MEANT WAS I'M NOT A THREAT.
THESE LANDS AND THE PEOPLE OF THE OLD WORLD WILL BENEFIT IN THE SHALLOW WAY OF THE NEW HUMAN BY THE GENEROSITY OF THE ELDER WHEN HE DIES.
I SWORE TO PROTECT HIM FROM HARM UNTIL HE RETURNS TO THE DREAMING.

IF I SWALLOWED A HIVE OF BEES, THEIR BUZZING IN MY HEAD WOULD BE LESS ANNOYING THAN YOUR PRATTLE.

WELL, THAT'S JUST RUDE.

AND THAT WAS WHEN I RECALLED SOMETHING BLACKSMITH HAD TOLD ME...
...HOW, TO NATIVE AUSTRALIANS, THE EARTH, THE PEOPLE, THE WORLD...HOW EVERYTHING IS ONE WITHIN THE DREAMING.
HOW, IN THE DREAMING, MY ETERNAL SPIRIT-CHILD EXISTS, ALONG WITH EVERYONE'S, BEFORE BIRTH ON EARTH AND AFTER DEATH.

HERE. SEE. SENSE. NOT AN ACT OF AGGRESSION...
IT IS THAT PART OF ME THAT REACHES OUT NOW.
...AN ACT OF FAITH.
I CAN BUT HOPE THE MANGAR-KUNJER-KUNJA FEELS THIS AND ANSWERS IN THE MANNER I REQUIRE OF HIM.
DIABLO BLACKSMITH WOULD TELL ME LATER THAT I HAD PERFORMED "SWAN DREAMING."
AT LEAST I THINK THAT'S WHAT HE SAID.
YOUR LIFEPATH, LIKE A RIVER MATING TIME, HAS VEERED.

EVIL YOU ARE. GOOD YOU ARE, TOO.
ENTER.

I'M NERVOUS.

WHY AM I NERVOUS?

IT'S NOT LIKE WE DON'T KNOW EACH OTHER...NOT LIKE WE HAVEN'T MET BEFORE.

STILL AND ALL...

...THAT **WAS** A LONG TIME AGO.
HELLO, DARNELL.
HELLO, GRANDFATHER.

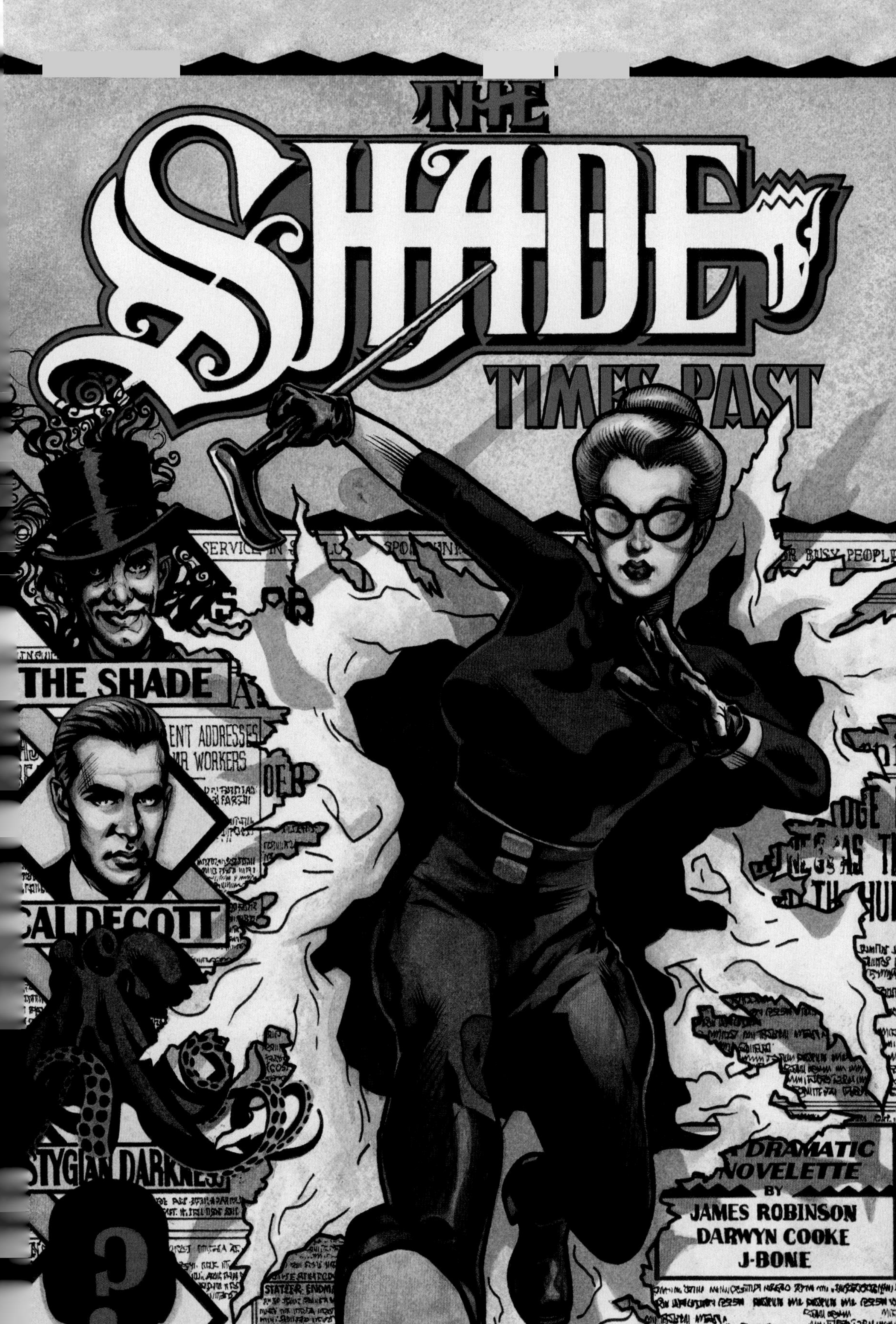
THE SHADE
TIMES PAST
THE SHADE
CALDECOTT
STYGIAN DARKNESS
MYSTERY MAN
A DRAMATIC NOVELETTE BY
JAMES ROBINSON
DARWYN COOKE
J-BONE

The Shade #4 variant cover art by Darwyn Cooke

It was April 14, 1944. And I confess, until that day, my only anti-German act had been abstaining from Pumpernickel.

Although if I am honest, I didn't like the bread and hadn't had a bite since long before Mr. Hitler began his litany of unpleasant behavior, so even this action was hardly the epitome of Anglo/American support.
This, despite the second great war of the world burning merrily far and wide.

I had long before taken the moniker "Shade" to conceal my true name, for no reason other than I'd wanted a farewell to whatever sense of humanity—ever small—I had left.
But it was only of late I'd begun to use it as...
...a stage name?
...a title?

Now, more and more I was "The Shade," and my crimes (in the past I think more a product of amorality than design) were becoming more calculated and steadfast.
In fact, it was in the orchestrating of one such enterprise that by happenstance I found myself in the events I now relate.
I suppose it began (as best I can recall) by my stepping out into the streets of Opal City.

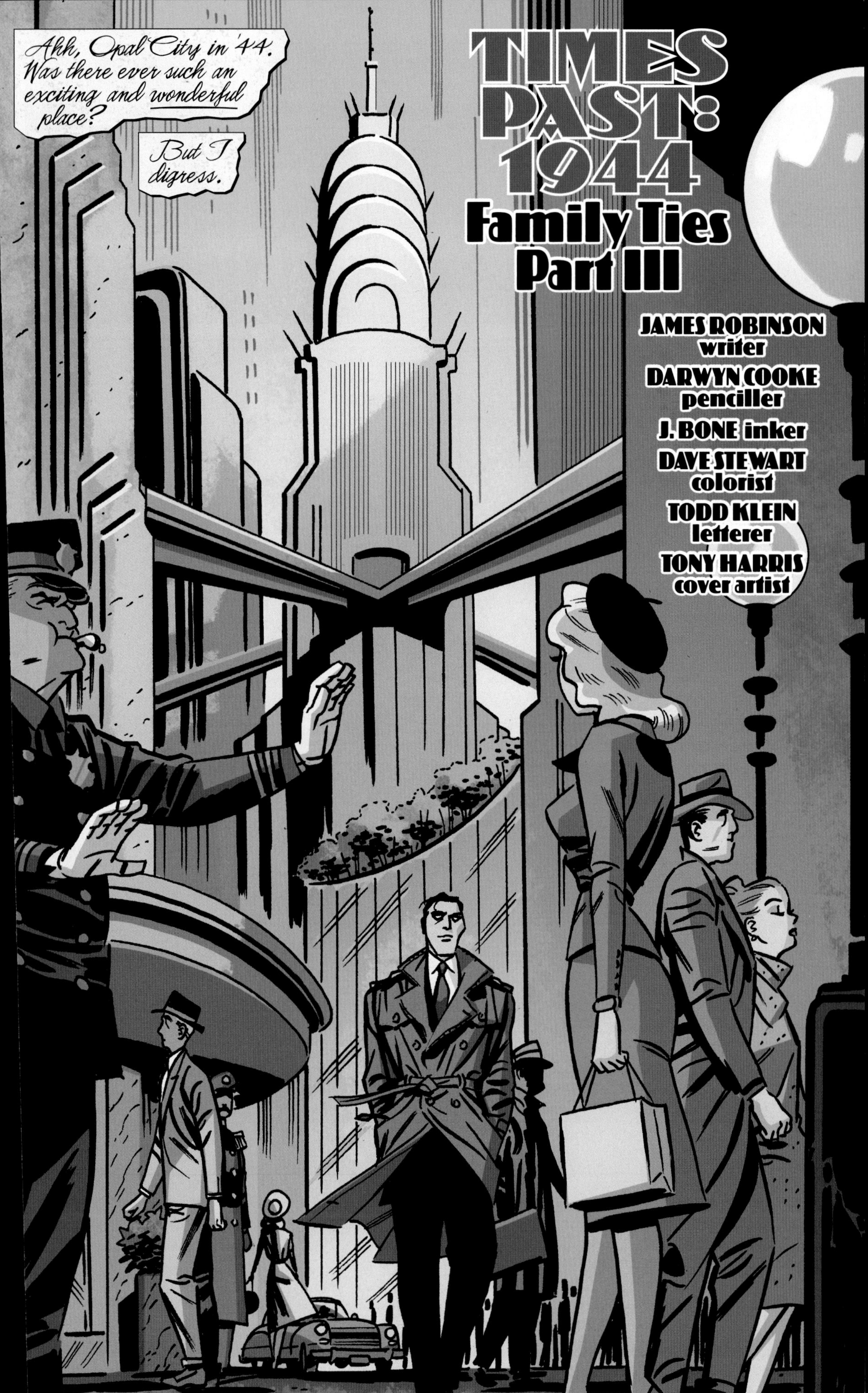
Ahh, Opal City in '44. Was there ever such an exciting and wonderful place?
But I digress.
TIMES PAST: 1944
Family Ties Part III
JAMES ROBINSON writer
DARWYN COOKE penciller
J. BONE inker
DAVE STEWART colorist
TODD KLEIN letterer
TONY HARRIS cover artist

THEN LET'S PRETEND THAT *IS* WHAT I WANT TO KNOW.

...that I suddenly became a patriot.

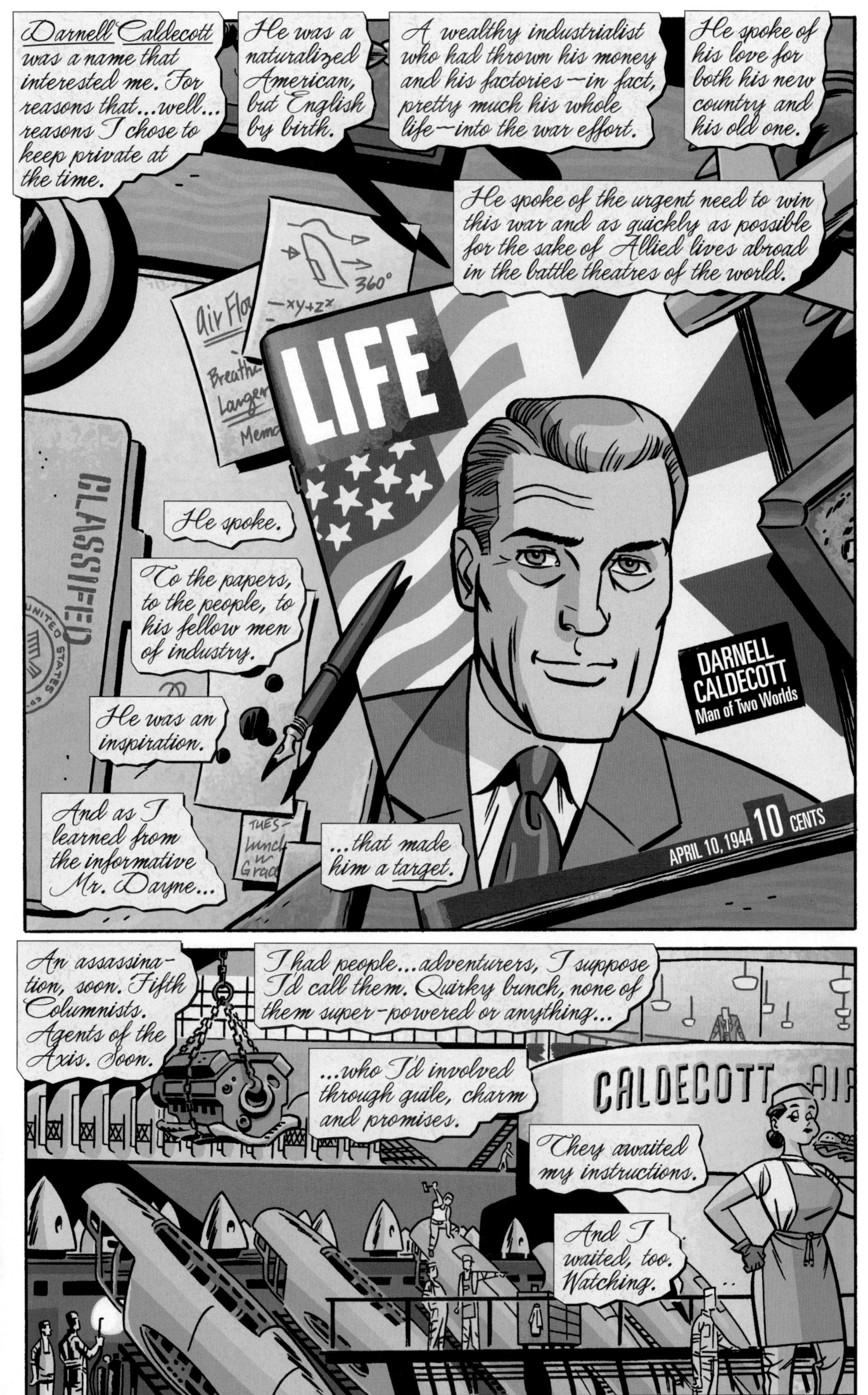
Darnell Caldecott was a name that interested me. For reasons that...well... reasons I chose to keep private at the time.
He was a naturalized American, but English by birth.
A wealthy industrialist who had thrown his money and his factories—in fact, pretty much his whole life—into the war effort.
He spoke of his love for both his new country and his old one.
He spoke of the urgent need to win this war and as quickly as possible for the sake of Allied lives abroad in the battle theatres of the world.
LIFE
CLASSIFIED
He spoke.
To the papers, to the people, to his fellow men of industry.
He was an inspiration.
DARNELL CALDECOTT
Man of Two Worlds
And as I learned from the informative Mr. Dayne...
...that made him a target.
APRIL 10, 1944
10 CENTS
An assassination, soon. Fifth Columnists. Agents of the Axis. Soon.
I had people...adventurers, I suppose I'd call them. Quirky bunch, none of them super-powered or anything...
...who I'd involved through guile, charm and promises.
CALDECOTT
They awaited my instructions.
And I waited, too. Watching.

LOOK, THERE'S NOTHING MORE TO SAY ON THE MATTER-- YOU CAN'T STAY HERE, DARNELL. NOT ANYMORE.
YES, YES. NEXT WEEK. I'LL LEAVE THEN. MAYBE.
THE WARNING WE RECEIVED WAS PRETTY CLEAR. I DO WISH YOU'D TAKE IT MORE SERIOUSLY.

I'M IN DANGER. I GATHER THAT.
BUT SO ARE THE BRAVE BOYS FIGHTING THIS WAR.
AND IF THE NAZIS WANT MY BLOOD TOO, THEN I GUESS I'M DOING SOMETHING RIGHT.
I REALLY FEEL MY PLACE IS HERE AT THE FACTORY, OR IF NOT, THEN OVER-SEEING THE Z44'S COMPLETION AND TESTING.

AH, MISS SHARP.
YOU WANTED ME, MR. CALDE-COTT?

DID WILL KNUDSEN GET BACK TO US? ABOUT MY MEETING WITH HIM?
NOT YET.
TRY AGAIN, WILL YOU? OR ARRANGE A CALL, HIM AND ME. I HAVE SOME IDEAS FOR MILITARY VEHICLES I'D LIKE TO THROW HIS WAY, SO--

OH, AND HOW RUDE OF ME. DARLING, YOU HAVEN'T MET MISS SHARP, HAVE YOU. MISS SHARP, THIS IS MY WIFE, GRACE.
HELLO.
H...HELLO.
MISS SHARP'S ONLY BEEN WITH ME THIS PAST FORTNIGHT, AND SHE'S ALREADY PROVING HER WORTH.

I'M HAPPY TO MEET YOU, MISS SHARP.
ME TOO, MRS. CALDECOTT.
AND I WISH I HAD MORE TIME FOR PLEASANTRIES, BUT I'M SIMPLY TOO WORRIED ABOUT DARNELL.

OH, FOR GOD'S SAKE. THE SUBJECT'S CLOSED, GRACE.
HONEY, YOU **HAVE** TO GET AWAY. THE F.B.I. ARE INSISTING. A SAFE HOUSE HAS BEEN ARRANGED. IT'S ALL SET. PLEASE.
BUT MY WORK--
PLEASE! AT LEAST UNTIL THEY'VE DEALT WITH THIS THREAT TO YOU. IT'S FOR THE BEST AND YOU KNOW IT.
Victo
THROU
PRODU

MISS SHARP, WILL YOU TRY TO REASON WITH HIM?
WELL...ERR...I **DO** THINK YOU'LL DO **MORE** FOR THE WAR EFFORT ALIVE THAN DEAD, SIR.
ALL RIGHT THEN, MISS SHARP--WOULD YOU ACCOMPANY ME TO THIS "SECRET HIDEAWAY"? DON'T WORRY, YOU'LL BE SAFE, LOTS OF G-MEN. AND WITH YOU THERE, AT LEAST I'LL BE ABLE TO GET THINGS ACCOMPLISHED.

OF COURSE, MR. CALDECOTT.
ANYTHING I CAN DO TO HELP.
SO YOU **ARE** GOING, DARNELL? THANK HEAVENS.

It was later...
...two days as near as the authorities could tell...that Caldecott's wife went missing.
The hunt was on. To little avail.
Which, I suppose, is where I should introduce one of the adventurers abetting me...

The Vigilante.

Where do I begin?

Two-fisted cowboy on a motorcycle.

Odd ensemble, but surprisingly effective.

And in his own fashion...
WHERE?!

...full of flash and color and not one whit of subtlety...
WHERE IS SHE?!

...he came through.
I'LL. TELL. JUST. DON'T. HIT. ME. AGAIN.

A location.
SY
ZEUS
MALTING

PLEASE, PLEASE. NO MORE. I'LL TELL YOU.

WHERE THEY'RE HIDING MY HUSBAND--I'LL TELL YOU.
1939

NO, MA'AM.
DON'T SUPPOSE YOU'LL HAVE TO.

NOT WHEN I'M **DONE** WITH THESE NAZI VARMINTS.

THERE. SAFE.

I *ALWAYS* HAVE BEEN.

MRS. CALDECOTT? MA'AM? I DON'T...
...UNDERSTAND. THIS. YOU'RE IN LEAGUE WITH THIS? YOU'RE A *NAZI?*

NOTHING OF THE KIND, BUT I KNOW WHAT'S *BEST* FOR ME. MY HUSBAND'S PATRIOTISM CUT INTO HIS COMPANY'S PROFITS.
HE DIES, THESE NAZIS ARE HAPPY. AND MY GETTING HIS FORTUNE MEANS I AM, *TOO.*

ALL THOSE PUNCHES THROWN... QUESTIONS ASKED BY YOU ALL OVER TOWN, WE KNEW YOU'D BE ALONG. THIS ROOM WAS WIRED TO WARN US WHEN YOU ARRIVED.
MY "INTERROGATION" WAS A LURE. BAITED, SET, AND HERE YOU ARE, RABBIT.
OH, WORD TO THE WISE: RUNNING ON ROOFTOPS IN THOSE SIZE 11 BOOTS OF YOURS...FAR FROM STEALTHY.
NOT THAT YOU'LL NEED MY ADVICE WHEN YOU'RE DEAD AND--

MY, BUT YOU'RE QUITE THE CHATTY ONE. SO CHAT...THESE NAZIS ABOUT US, THIS CAN'T BE ALL OF THEM. NO, I'D GUESS MORE.
WHERE?

YOU KNOW YOUR HUSBAND'S LOCATION. DO THEY KNOW? HAVE YOU TOLD THEM?
YOU CLAIM TO KNOW WHAT'S BEST FOR YOU? HMM. I'D SAY AT THIS MOMENT YOU SPEAKING UP IS SLIGHTLY MORE ADVANTAGEOUS THAN DYING.

WHICH YOU ARE OH SO CLOSE TO DOING.
NO, NO... I'LL TELL YOU... I...A...

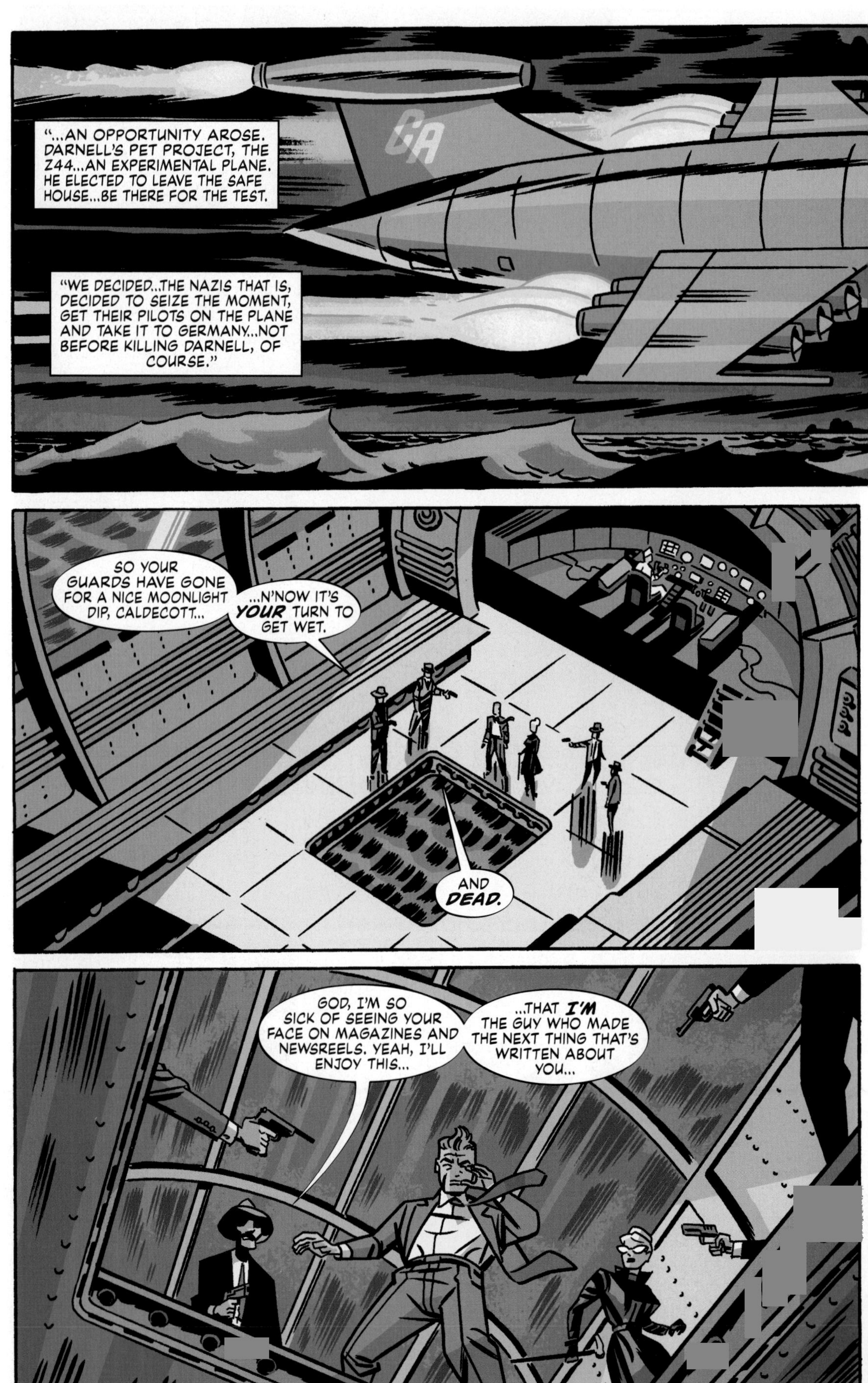

"...AN OPPORTUNITY AROSE. DARNELL'S PET PROJECT, THE Z44...AN EXPERIMENTAL PLANE. HE ELECTED TO LEAVE THE SAFE HOUSE...BE THERE FOR THE TEST.
"WE DECIDED...THE NAZIS THAT IS, DECIDED TO SEIZE THE MOMENT, GET THEIR PILOTS ON THE PLANE AND TAKE IT TO GERMANY...NOT BEFORE KILLING DARNELL, OF COURSE."
SO YOUR GUARDS HAVE GONE FOR A NICE MOONLIGHT DIP, CALDECOTT...
...N'NOW IT'S ***YOUR*** TURN TO GET WET.
AND ***DEAD.***
GOD, I'M SO SICK OF SEEING YOUR FACE ON MAGAZINES AND NEWSREELS. YEAH, I'LL ENJOY THIS...
...THAT ***I'M*** THE GUY WHO MADE THE NEXT THING THAT'S WRITTEN ABOUT YOU...

...YOUR OBITUARY.
STAY BACK, MISS SHARP! GET BEHIND ME! PERHAPS THEY'LL SPARE YOU IF--

NO, MR. CALDECOTT! YOU GET BEHIND ME!

I'LL PROTECT YOU!
I present to you... Madam Fatal.
Richard Stanton, retired actor, using the guise of a woman to fight crime.
Yes, indeed, where do I begin with this one, too?
Of course, in my varied (and some might say tawdry) travels, I've encountered that breed of men who enjoy wearing women's clothing.
But the activities of such fellows normally involve cocktails and torch songs—
—not punching spies and yegg men.

WILL SOMEBODY SHOOT THIS DAME? SHE'S GOING TO MESS UP EVERYTHI--

THERE. ALL DONE.

I DON'T... UNDERSTAND. MISS SHARP? YOU'RE--?

NOT WHAT I APPEARED TO BE. I'M SORRY FOR THE SUBTERFUGE.
I...I DON'T KNOW WHAT TO SAY.

THEN WHY DON'T I SPEAK FOR THE MOMENT, DARNELL. THERE'S MORE YOU SHOULD KNOW ABOUT THIS...YOUR WIFE--
GRACE? WHAT ABOUT HER?
IN A MOMENT. FIRST...

HERE, STANTON, AS PROMISED...THE LOCATION OF YOUR DAUGHTER. TRICKY, BUT I FOUND IT. CHAP NAMED DR. PROWL, OLD FOE OF YOURS, APPARENTLY...HE TOOK SOME "CONVINCING" TO COUGH IT UP.
And with that, one man's quest of eleven years ends.
THANK YOU, SHADE. OH MY GOD...I CAN'T BELIEVE IT.

AND NOW, DARNELL, I SUGGEST YOU LAND THIS TOY OF YOURS.
YOU AND I SHOULD TALK.

Later. Dawn and a beach that offers us seclusion...
...as I reveal...

OH, GRACE. YOU STUPID, SILLY FOOL.
YOU'LL DIVORCE HER, OF COURSE.
HIRE LAWYERS FOR THAT.
OTHER LAWYERS TO DEFEND HER FROM THE INEVITABLE TREASON CHARGE. LOTS OF LAWYERS.

ARE YOU WHO I THINK YOU ARE?
AND WHO WOULD THAT BE?
YOU'RE THE FAMILY SECRET, YES? YOU'RE MY GREAT-GRANDFATHER.

GUILTY.

WE TALK ABOUT YOU...OF YOU... THE FAMILY DOES. AT BIG GATHERINGS. WE WONDER ABOUT YOUR LIFE. WHETHER IT'S TRUE ABOUT THE POWERS YOU HAVE.
WELL, YOU CAN NOW ATTEST TO THEM, I'D SAY.

BUT YOU KNOW THE QUESTION WE ASK THE MOST? *WHY* DOESN'T HE COMMUNICATE WITH US...?

...*WHY* ARE YOU A STRANGER TO YOUR OWN BLOOD?
A PIECE OF ME DIED THE DAY I BECAME WHAT I AM NOW. I FEARED FOR THE SAFETY OF MY WIFE THEN...YOUR GREAT-GRAND-MOTHER.

SHE SPOKE OF YOU OFTEN. I THINK SHE STAYED IN LOVE WITH YOU UNTIL SHE DIED.
THAT MAKES ME SAD TO KNOW.

SORRY. I DIDN'T MEAN TO--OH, AND SHE SAW YOU ONCE. WHEN SHE WAS VERY OLD. 1900 OR THEREABOUTS.
1901. AND I DIDN'T REALIZE SHE WAS AWARE I WAS THERE.

WHY DID YOU CHOOSE TO SAVE ME?
YOU'RE MY DESCENDANT, HOW COULD I NOT? I...WANT YOU TO KNOW, BY THE WAY...ALL YOU'RE DOING. THE WAR. I'M PROUD OF YOU.

I HAVE TO GO.
SO SOON?
THERE'S SO *MUCH* I WANT TO ASK. FOR THE FAMILY.

OH YES, THE GATHERINGS YOU SPOKE OF.
WELL, I SUPPOSE I COULD STAY A WHILE LONGER.
LET'S WALK ON. ASK ME WHAT YOU WANT AND I'LL ANSWER THE THINGS I THINK YOU SHOULD KNOW.

WELL FIRSTLY, HOW DID YOU BECOME WHAT YOU ARE TODAY?
I CAN'T ANSWER THAT.
HMM. THIS IS GOING WELL.
SWIMMINGLY.

THEN TELL ME SOME OF THE PLACES YOU'VE SEEN. WHERE'S THE MOST EXOTIC?
HUH. I SUPPOSE THAT WOULD BE IN 1903, THE TIME A SCIENCE-HERO FELLOW I KNEW...WALDO GLENMORGAN-- WE TOOK AN EXPEDITION TO A PLACE CALLED SKARTARIS.
NOW, THAT LAND WAS INCREDIBLE. YOU WOULDN'T BELIEVE...

But that's a story for another time.
Darnell and I walked and talked for a good hour before I took my leave.
The next time I saw him, in Australia...
...was at his deathbed.

The Shade #5 variant cover art by Javier Pulido

HOW CAN YOU GO ON LIVING ***KNOWING*** WHAT YOU ARE?

HOW CAN YOU NOT TAKE THE KNIFE TO YOUR THROAT? NO, I FORGET, SUCH A THING WOULDN'T KILL YOU. WHY, THE WOUND WOULD HEAL AS QUICKLY AS IT FORMED.

BUT A STAKE TO THE HEART. THAT WOULD WORK.

OR SUNLIGHT.

HOW CAN YOU ***BEAR*** TO EXIST, ***KNOWING*** WHAT YOU ARE?

DEAD.

A DEAD ***THING...***

...A *VAMPIRE.*

YOU DON'T SCARE ME, ***MONSTER!***

YES, THESE VILLAINS, ***LOS TOMADORES...*** "THE TAKERS"... THEY WALK THE PATH OF GREED, THEY SIN. ONE OF THE SEVEN DEADLY, GREED, YES, YES...

...BUT YOU ***TRANSCEND*** THAT. SIN? WHY, YOU ARE ***EVIL PERSONIFIED.***

LA SANGRE. "THE BLOOD."

I SPIT ON THE PEOPLE WHO CROWN YOU THEIR HERO... THEIR CHAMPION. THEY OF THE "CIUTAT VELLA" WHO CALL YOU "VERGE DE LA NIT."

HEROINE QUEEN OF BARCELONA, PROTECTOR OF CATALONIA.

I SPIT ON THOSE FOOLS, FOR TO LOVE YOU IS TO LOVE ***DAMNATION.***

...BIFOCALS, PERHAPS.

BARCELONA HAS ALWAYS BEEN ONE OF MY FAVORITE PORTS OF CALL.

AND TONIGHT IS NO EXCEPTION.

MEMORIA ROJA

JAMES ROBINSON writer
JAVIER PULIDO artist
HILARY SYCAMORE colorist
TODD KLEIN letterer
TONY HARRIS cover artist

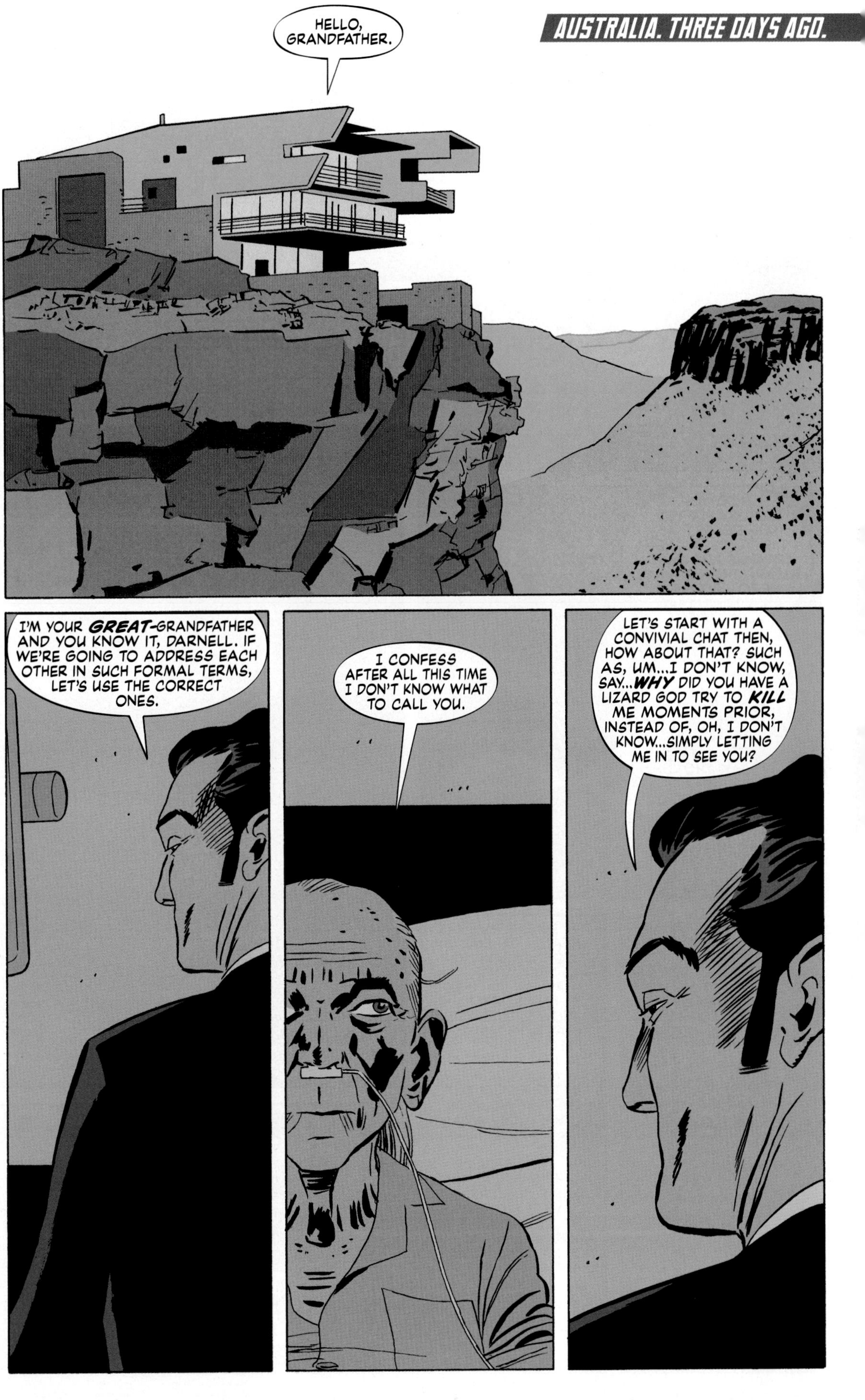

AUSTRALIA. THREE DAYS AGO.

HELLO, GRANDFATHER.

NOT SURE WHY IT ATTACKED YOU, HONESTLY. DON'T KNOW. I'M SORRY IF--
WELL, I THINK IT WAS PROBABLY ME... MY DARKNESS SCARED THE CREATURE. BUT ENOUGH WITH "SORRY," DARNELL, MY BOY, WHAT IS GOING ON? I WAS ATTACKED IN MY HOME.
AND LATER I MET A GERMAN PRIVATE DETECTIVE--
VON HAMMER.

VON HAMMER, THAT'S RIGHT. HE SAID HE'D BEEN HIRED BY YOU TO LOCATE BLOOD SAMPLES OF MINE.
WHY? WHY IN GOD'S NAME?

LUCKY YOU. LUCK DAMN YOU. YOU DESERT US, THE FAMILY. ALL YOU LEAVE US ARE TALES... VILLAIN, THIEF, MANIAC, HERO--BIT OF A SURPRISE, THAT LAST ONE...
ASS, I SAY. THOUGHTLESS, SELFISH ASS. LEAVING US WITHOUT--
COUGH

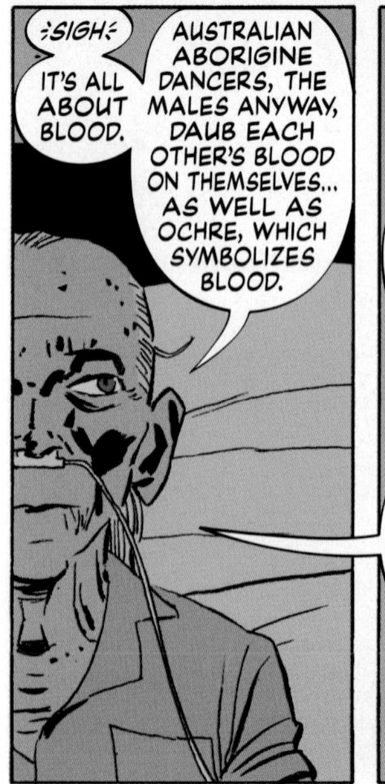
SIGH
IT'S ALL ABOUT BLOOD.
AUSTRALIAN ABORIGINE DANCERS, THE MALES ANYWAY, DAUB EACH OTHER'S BLOOD ON THEMSELVES... AS WELL AS OCHRE, WHICH SYMBOLIZES BLOOD.
THEY BELIEVE THE BLOOD CREATES AN ENERGY CONNECTION TO DREAMTIME.
AND I DON'T KNOW I DISAGREE, WHAT WITH THE IRON IN BLOOD, OCHRE TOO FOR THAT MATTER, AND THE MAGNETIC FIELDS IN THE WORLD. BUT I'M DRIFTING...I DO THAT MORE AND MORE.
YOU BECAME THE SHADE IN 1838. AND FOR SOME YEARS YOU WERE A SUPERHUMAN... AND I STRESS THE WORD HUMAN. YOU HAD BLOOD. YOU HAD THE PHYSIOLOGY OF A MAN, BUT WITH SHADOWY POWERS.

THEN SOMETHING HAPPENED A FEW YEARS LATER ON...NO, "A FEW" IS WRONG. TWENTY YEARS ON, YOU CHANGED.
HEAVENS, YOU KNOW MORE ABOUT THIS THAN I DO.

YOUR POWERS PERHAPS CONSUMED YOU...ERODED YOUR HUMANITY.

I'M DYING. BVIOUS LOOKING AT ME, RIGHT?
ERR, I CONFESS YOU'VE LOOKED BETTER.
LEUKEMIA. OLD MAN'S LEUKEMIA. NOT THAT IT'S SO DIFFERENT FROM A CHILD'S, EXCEPT THE RIGORS OF THERAPY... MY DECREPIT FRAME ISN'T UP TO IT.
NOT SO BAD A DEATH, REALLY. CANCER'S MORE PAINFUL. ALZHEIMER'S STEALS DIGNITY. HEART ATTACK, STROKE--NO TIME TO PLAN.
DON'T SUPPOSE YOU'VE EVER THOUGHT ABOUT SUCH THINGS, EH, GRANDFATHER? NEVER HAD TO.
ERR... NO.
I'M SORRY. I'M NOT ANGRY, I'M...NO, I AM ANGRY, JUST NOT AT YOU.
THEN WHO? DARNELL, YOU HAVEN'T TOLD ME ANYTHING YET.
IT'S SOMEONE IN THE FAMILY.
DARNELL, THAT LIST OF THINGS YOU SAID ABOUT ME IS RIGHT. WAS, ANYWAY. BUT I'M HERE NOW AND I WANT TO MAKE AMENDS.
YES, I SEE.
YES, YOU KEEP SAYING THAT, AND YOU'VE ALSO ATTESTED TO YOUR OWN MORTALITY, SO I'M GUESSING YOU'RE TRYING TO ACQUIRE SOME MEANS VIA OUR GENETIC LINK TO PROLONG YOUR LIFE. IMMORTALITY--
ACTUALLY, IT WAS SOMETHING ELSE...AN UTSIDE FACTOR. UT IT'S OF LITTLE MATTER--GO ON.
YOU NO LONGER HAVE BLOOD IN THE CONVENTIONAL SENSE, MERELY DARK ESSENCE.
AND IT'S YOUR BLOOD THAT I NEED.
--IS OVERRATED.
DEATH? I WELCOME IT, THE PEACE...BE IT HEAVEN'S CHORUS OR BLACK OBLIVION. NO, I SEEK TO MERELY FORESTALL MY PASSING UNTIL I CAN ANSWER A FEW QUESTIONS.

AS I'M SURE YOU MIGHT SURMISE...

...LA SANGRE AND I HAVE A HISTORY.

YOU STILL HAVE THAT COLLECTION OF YOURS?

OF COURSE, BIGGER THAN EVER. JUST ACQUIRED SOME J.F.K. AND ALFRED HITCHCOCK.

EVERYONE NEEDS A HOBBY, I SUPPOSE.

YES, FATHER.

I'M NOT YOUR FATHER, I'VE TOLD YOU THAT I DON'T KNOW ***HOW*** MANY TIMES. CALL ME RICHARD.

BUT ANYWAY, TELL ME, CHILD...

...DO YOU BY CHANCE, BURIED SOMEWHERE DEEP WITHIN THIS COLLECTION OF YOURS...

...HAVE ANY BLOOD OF ***MINE?***

A VIAL, YOU SAY, MY STUBBORN GIRL? WHY, A VIAL WILL DO THE TRICK. LET US AWAY.

LEAVE THIS MESS FOR THE POLICIA NACIONAL TO HOSE DOWN, WHY NOT? COME.

YOU KNOW, FATHER, I THINK I JUST MIGHT. A VIAL.

NOT WHAT I WAS EXPECTING, BUT VERY PLEASANT.

I MOVE WITH THE TIMES.

WHEN I SPORTED THE LONG CAPE AND PETTICOATS, SO TOO DID MOST THE WORLD OVER. AND MY HOME THEN--

THAT MANSION, QUITE. ALL THOSE CANDLES AND COBWEBS.

--WAS GOTHIC BECAUSE SUCH WAS THE ERA.

--THAT THE TAKERS HAVE BEEN DEFEATED BY LA SANGRE AFTER THEIR REIGN OF TERROR OVER BARCELONA, WHICH HAD LEFT THIRTY-SEVEN DEAD.

THE PARENTS OF RAUL PINA, THE LAST OF THE KIDNAPPED CHILDREN, SAID THAT ALTHOUGH THIS WOULDN'T BRING THEIR DEAD SON BACK, THEY THANKED THE CITY'S CHAMPION AND DEFENDER FOR AT LEAST BRINGING RAUL'S KILLERS TO JUSTICE.

THEY LOVE YOU. THE PEOPLE OF BARCELONA. I'M GLAD. I FEARED FOR YOU WHEN WE...UH...FIRST MET. THAT YOU'D BE CURSED WITH AN EXISTENCE OF LONELY SORROW, BUT IT'S NOT LIKE THAT AT ALL.
YES, AND I'D DIE FOR THEM IF I HAD TO. THE FEELING'S MUTUAL.

NOW, ABOUT YOU, FATHER. YOUR BLOOD. THIS ALL SOUNDS VERY MYSTERIOUS AND EXCITING. TELL ME--NO...HOLD ON, WAIT--
--AND ALMOST IMMEDIATELY FOLLOWING THE NEWS OF LA SANGRE'S VICTORY, ANOTHER THREAT HAS ARISEN, ONE ALL TOO FAMILIAR TO BOTH HER AND THIS CITY...

...THE INQUISITOR HAS RETURNED.
ZONY
I SEE HER CHANGE. ALERT. HER HANDS ARE SHAKING, BARELY, BUT--

THIS FELLOW, HE'S-- YOU'VE MET HIM BEFORE, YES? I RECALL READING TALES... NEWS FROM SPAIN DOESN'T REACH AMERICA SO READILY, BUT I'M SURE I'VE HEARD THE NAME.
THE INQUISITOR...

"...HE'S MY ARCHENEMY. MY SUPREME FOE.

"WARRIOR PRIEST, ZEALOT, MANIAC. HE DESPISES ANY SINNER, NO MATTER THE SIZE OR CIRCUMSTANCE OF THE INFRACTION.

"HE'D KILL A MURDERER OR A RAPIST, A PETTY THIEF... EVEN A LIAR, AND SEE NO DIFFERENCE. YOU CAN IMAGINE WHAT HE PERCEIVES ***I*** REPRESENT.

"FROM HIS ***DEMENTED*** PERSPECTIVE, I'M HELL-SPAWNED.

"WE'VE BEEN CROSSING PATHS, ON AND OFF, SINCE JUST BEFORE THE GREAT WAR."

"BARCELONA FASHION WEEK"-- WHAT IS THAT BUT A SHRINE TO VANITY, LUST AND JEALOUS GREED? A GOLDEN CALF FOR ME TO TOPPLE.
TO THIS END, I HAVE ASSEMBLED A FASHION COL-LECTION OF MY OWN.
AND BY THAT I MEAN THE MODELS AND DESIGNERS WHO I'VE SEIZED THESE EARLY HOURS. TWENTY-FIVE SOULS--QUITE THE COLLECTION INDEED--
--WHO I'LL BEGIN DISFIGURING AND KILLING WITHIN THE DAY...
ZONY

...IF YOUR CHAMPION, LA SANGRE, DOESN'T COME BEFORE ME AND TAKE HER OWN LIFE. SIMPLE.
BARCELONA, YOU HAVE THAT MUCH TIME AND NO MORE TO CONTACT LA SANGRE WITH MY DEMANDS.

AND AS AN INCENTIVE, TO ASSURE YOU OF MY GRAVITY...ONE OF THE MODELS CRIED TOO MUCH.

HERE IS HER FACE.

YOUR BLOOD WILL HAVE TO WAIT.
OF COURSE. ABSOLUTELY. WE'LL FIND THIS LUNATIC, KILL HIM, AND THEN--
NO, FATHER, HE'S MY FOE, MY THREAT. I DON'T WANT TO INVOLVE YOU.
BUT SANGRE, MY DEAR...

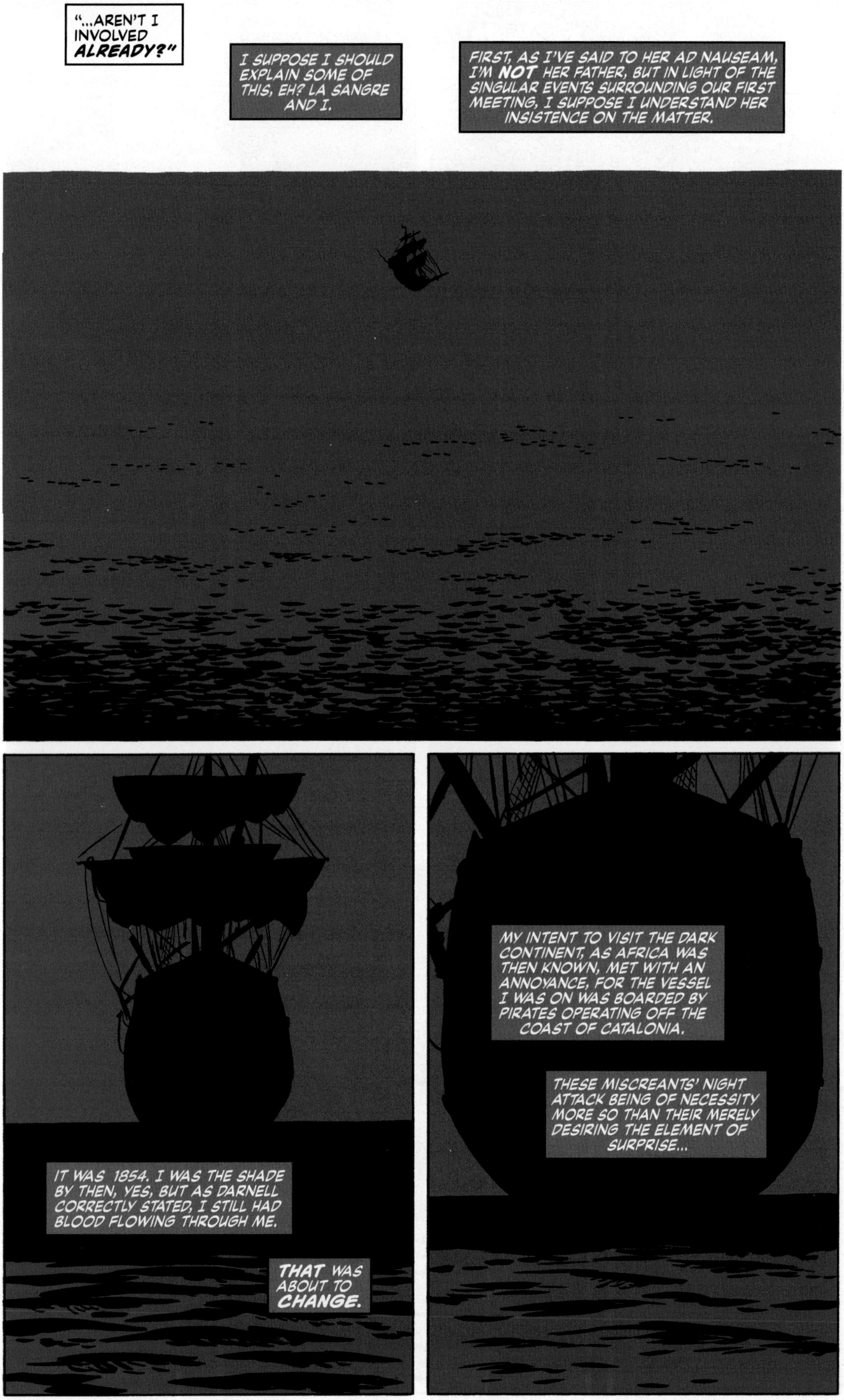

"...AREN'T I INVOLVED ***ALREADY?***"

I SUPPOSE I SHOULD EXPLAIN SOME OF THIS, EH? LA SANGRE AND I.

*FIRST, AS I'VE SAID TO HER AD NAUSEAM, I'M **NOT** HER FATHER, BUT IN LIGHT OF THE SINGULAR EVENTS SURROUNDING OUR FIRST MEETING, I SUPPOSE I UNDERSTAND HER INSISTENCE ON THE MATTER.*

...FOR THEY WERE VAMPIRES.

I WAS ROUSED FROM SLUMBER BY THE SCREAMS OF THE SHIP'S CREW AND THOSE OF MY FELLOW PASSENGERS--A JEWELER FROM BILBAO, HIS WIFE AND BABY DAUGHTER.

NOT ONE JOT.

I DIDN'T KNOW IF WHAT I ATTEMPTED WOULD WORK. I'D READ OF WAYS TO DEAL WITH SNAKE VENOM, OF COURSE...SNAKE BITES...
I THOUGHT PERHAPS I MIGHT HAVE THE SAME RESULT WITH THE POISON OF A VAMPIRE, IF I WAS IN TIME.

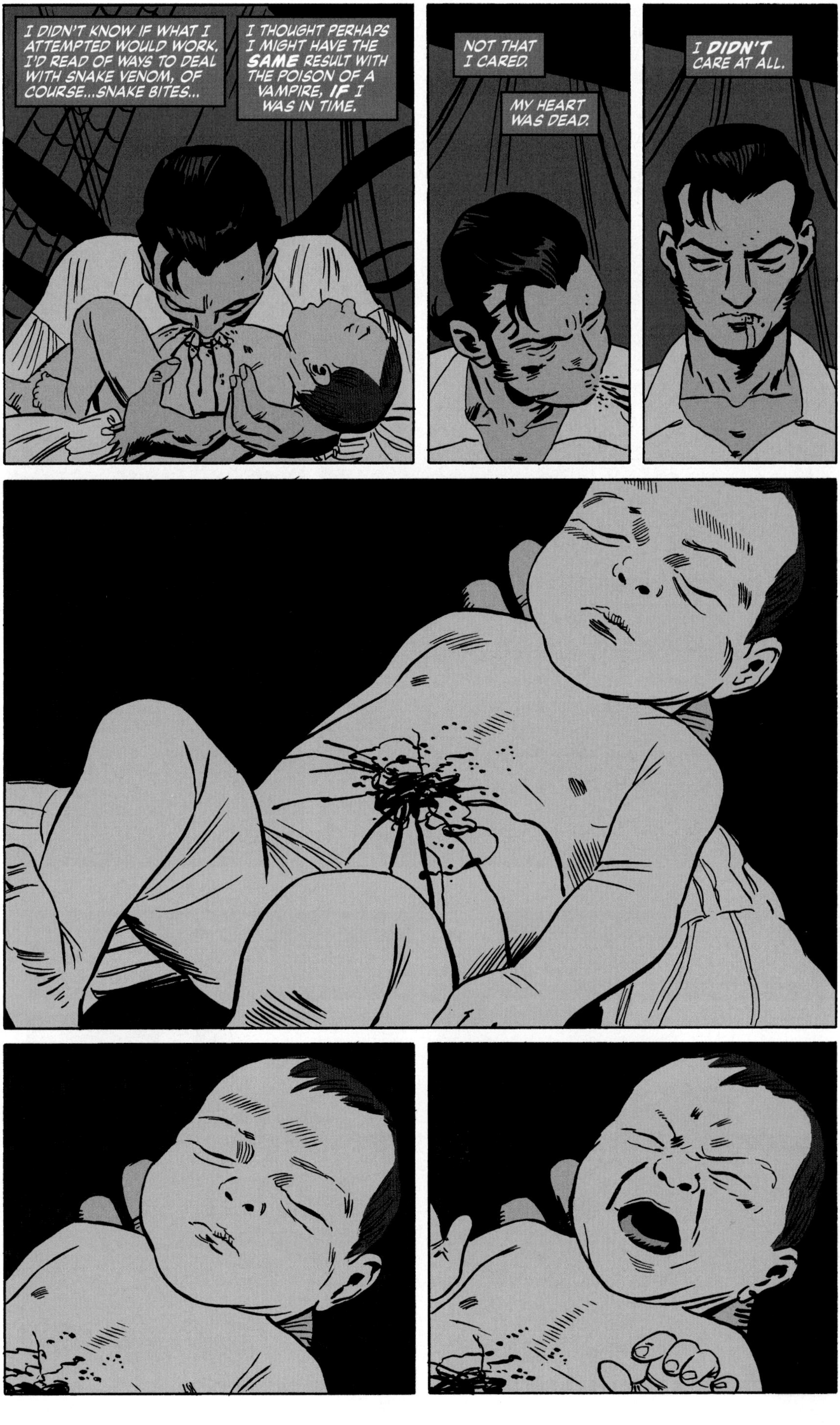

NOT THAT I CARED.
MY HEART WAS DEAD.

I DIDN'T CARE AT ALL.

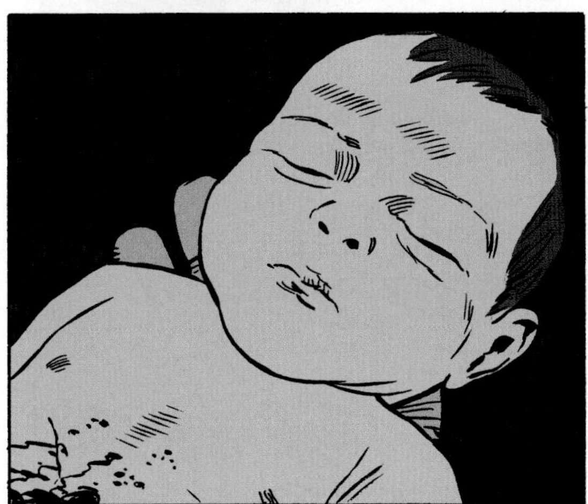

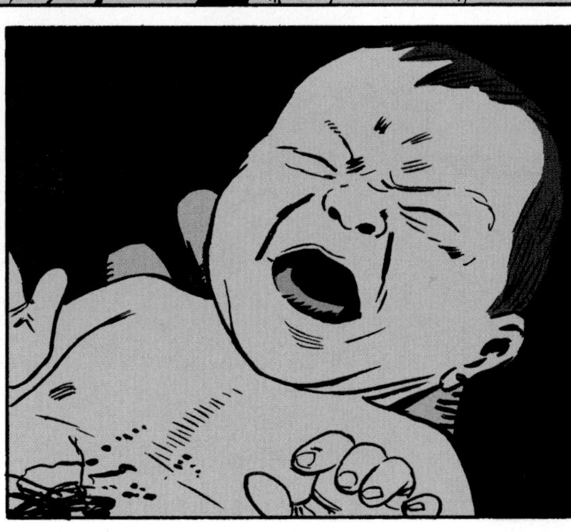

GO ON, HAVE A GOOD OLD CRY.

...UNTIL TODAY.
NO, FATHER, I'VE DECIDED I MUST DO THIS ALONE.
RICHARD. CALL ME RICHARD, HOW MANY TIMES MUST I TELL YOU?
FATHER.
STUBBORN CHILD.
ALONE, I SAY. THE INQUISITOR IS MY FOE, MY BANE. I'VE HANDLED HIM COUNTLESS TIMES. I DON'T NEED YOU COMING TO MY RESCUE.

NOT RESCUE. ASSISTANCE. AND PRIDE IS NOT A TRAIT I ADMIRE...IN YOU, ANYWAY. YOU'RE A PART OF MY LIFE AS I AM YOURS. DON'T BE A LITTLE FOOL.
LET'S ACT, AND QUICKLY BEFORE OTHERS LOSE THEIR FACES.
YOU'RE RIGHT. OF COURSE YOU ARE...IT'S JUST...
...THERE'S MORE TO THE INQUISITOR, THIS TIME. I FEAR HE'S...CHANGED. WHAT YOU ASKED ME A MOMENT AGO...HIS IMMORTALITY...THERE'S MORE TO HIM.
IT'S NOT JUST "STOP THE VILLAIN AND SAVE THE DAY" THIS TIME, THERE'S A MYSTERY HIDDEN AMONG THIS MADNESS, I KNOW IT.

THEN LEAD ON, MY DEAR...

...LET'S SOLVE IT TOGETHER!

The Shade #6 variant cover art by Javier Pulido

Las Cinco Esquinas

JAMES ROBINSON writer
JAVIER PULIDO artist
HILARY SYCAMORE colorist
TODD KLEIN letterer
TONY HARRIS cover artist

"NOW ***GO***...

"...FOR YOU ***KNOW*** WHAT YOU MUST ***DO***."

LA SANGRE. FAMED "LADY" OF THIS CITY~~

NO.

NO...

...MY LADY. I WILL DO IT, I ***SWEAR...***

1944.

DIE, WITCH! DEMON! ***WHORE!***

I...I AM NONE OF THOSE THINGS, VILLAIN. BUT YOU...

THUD

...YOU ARE NO GENTLEMAN!

...I WILL ***SAVE*** YOU YET.

COMISARIA GRANDE CATALUNYA.
IT NEVER CEASES TO AMAZE ME HOW ACCEPTING AND INDEED ALMOST REVERENT THE AUTHORITIES ARE TOWARDS MY FRIEND LA SANGRE, WHO IS, AFTER ALL...
...TO ALL INTENTS AND PURPOSES, A VAMPIRE.
BRAVO (OR SHOULD I SAY OLÉ?) TO LATIN MORES.
SO OF COURSE THIS IS AS MADDENING AND CONTRADICTORY AS EVERY OTHER TIME WITH THE INQUISITOR.
WHY, YOU SAID IT YOURSELF, MY LADY: "MADDENING." THE MAN IS A MANIAC.
PERHAPS IT'S HER DEVOUT FAITH. OR HOW SHE'S PROTECTED THIS CITY FOR MORE THAN A CENTURY. OR SIMPLY HER CHARMING MANNER?

HE TELLS ME HE WANTS ME TO SURRENDER MYSELF TO HIM, PRESUMABLY SO HE CAN KILL ME FINALLY, AND YET HE NEGLECTS TO TELL ME *WHERE* I SHOULD PRESENT MYSELF.

IT SEEMS TO ME THAT'S PART OF THE GAME, DON'T YOU THINK? "SURRENDER OR I KILL THE MODELS AND DESIGNERS I'VE KIDNAPPED... OH, BUT YOU HAVE TO FIND ME FIRST."

ALL I KNOW IS THAT LIVES ARE AT STAKE.
YES, BUT THESE LIVES AT THE COST OF YOUR OWN?...I HATE TO SAY IT, BUT--
THEN *DON'T,* COMMISSIONER CERVANTES--DON'T EVEN THINK IT. MY LIFE FOR THE LIVES OF MANY, THE CHOICE IS *CLEAR.* IF I *ONLY* KNEW WHERE THE INQUISITOR WAS.
IF THAT IS YOUR WISH...

...MAY ***I*** OFFER ASSISTANCE?

MONTPELLIER *MAKES HIS PRESENCE KNOWN WITH A CALMNESS MORE DRAMATIC THAN MANY A THUNDERSTORM.*

HONESTLY, I'M A TAD JEALOUS.

STANDING THERE LIKE THAT, ALONG WITH ANOTHER OF BARCELONA'S VILLAINS, "BROMA OSCURA" (WHO IN THIS PARTICULAR MOMENT IS CLEARLY NOT FINDING ANYTHING VERY FUNNY). YES, VERY STRIKING.

HOW GENEROUS. YOU COME BOTH OFFERING AID ***AND*** BEARING GIFTS. MY, BARCELONA IS A FRIENDLY PLACE.

SHADE, THIS IS MY SOME-TIMES PARTNER IN CRIME- FIGHTING, MONTPELLIER.

I KNOW OF YOU BY REPUTA-TION.

OH, DON'T BELIEVE ALL YOU MAY HAVE READ ABOUT MY WIT AND ÉLAN. NO, WAIT, COME TO THINK OF IT, PLEASE DO.

I KNOW OF YOU TOO, BY THE BY. YOU'RE A MAN OF ***MANY*** TALENTS.

MONTPELLIER, AS HIS NAME SUGGESTS, HAS SOME KIND OF SNAKY, SPEEDY FIGHTING ABILITY... BORN WITH IT, BY ALL ACCOUNTS. THE VENOM BLASTS HE USES ARE ARTIFICIAL, HOWEVER...'THOUGH I WOULDN'T AVER TO IT.

PLEASE FIND A CELL FOR THIS PIECE OF FILTH, AND TELL ME WHAT YOU KNOW SO FAR OF YOUR DILEMMA.
OF COURSE. ALTHOUGH I FEAR THE **FORMER** REQUEST IS FAR **EASIER** THAN THE LATTER.
BANGLADESHI BY BIRTH, BUT ARRIVING HERE AGED THREE, HE (QUITE ARDENTLY, IN FACT) CALLS HIMSELF A SPANIARD.
THE INTERESTING THING ABOUT HIM IS--

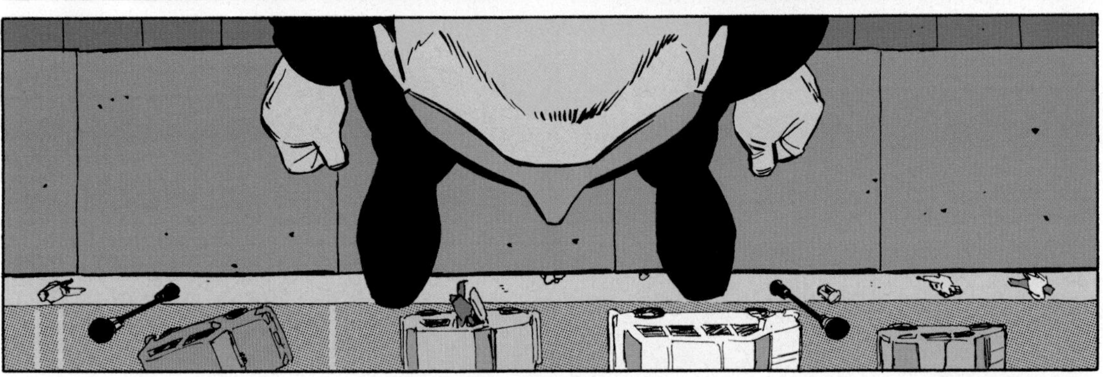

SIR, REPORT JUST IN...**FOUR** OF THE INQUISITOR'S **ACOLYTES...** ALL SUICIDAL...EACH IN A DIFFERENT PART OF THE CITY!

WHERE WAS I? OH YES...THE THING ABOUT MONTPELLIER IS THAT, APART FROM HIS REPTILIAN POWERS, HE'S THE "DETECTIVE" SUPERHERO OF SPAIN. THE SOLVER-OF-CRIMES TYPE...LIKE BATMAN, NIGHTWING AND SUCH.
FOUR? ARE YOU **SURE?** NOT **FIVE?**
WHAT ARE YOU SITTING HERE FOR, MEN? GET **OUT** THERE AND ROUND THOSE LUNATICS UP. MAYBE **THEY'LL** SHED SOME LIGHT ON--

BLAMMM
THAT'S THE THING, SIR. UM. I DON'T THINK THEY'LL HAVE MUCH TO SAY.

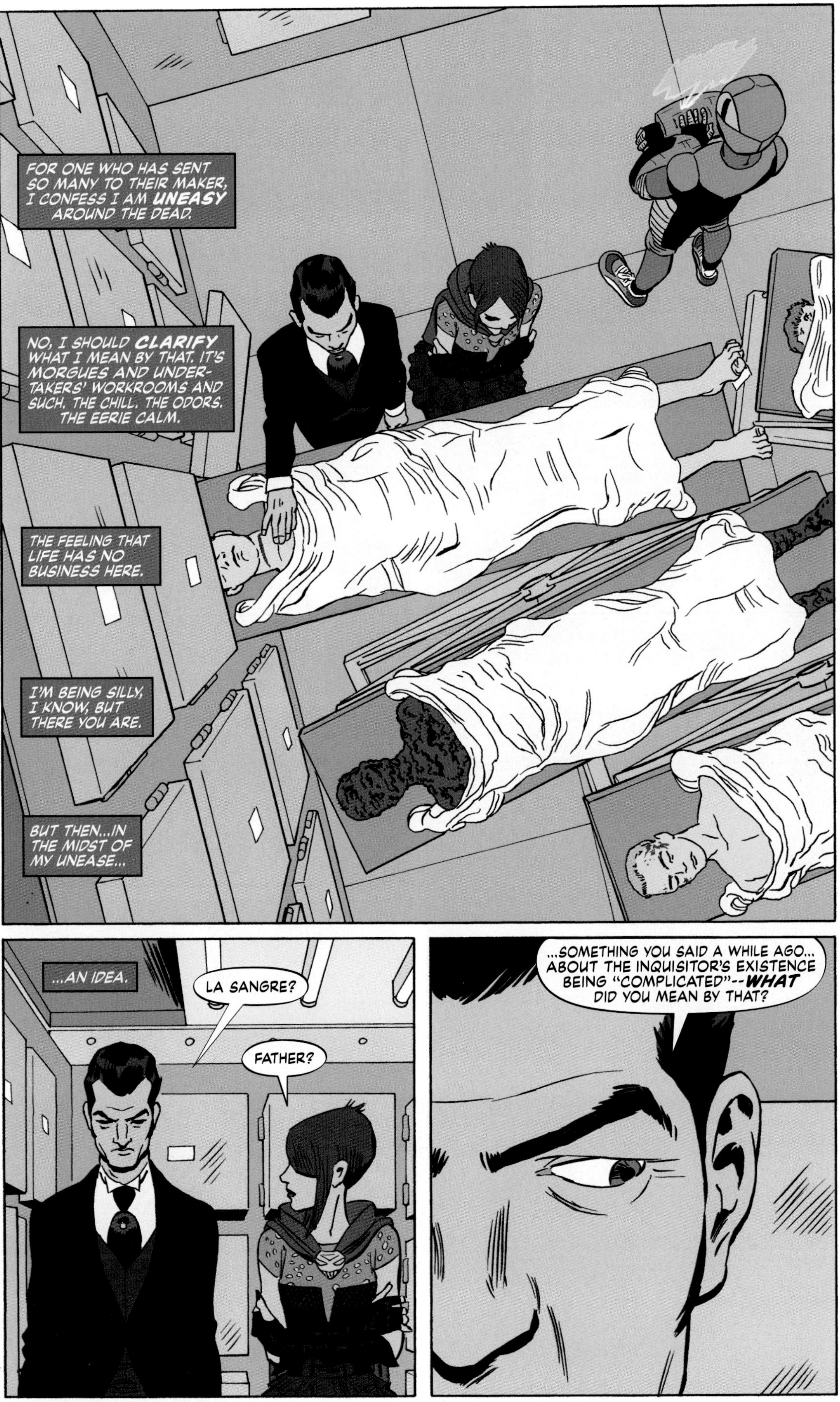

FOR ONE WHO HAS SENT SO MANY TO THEIR MAKER, I CONFESS I AM **UNEASY** AROUND THE DEAD.

NO, I SHOULD **CLARIFY** WHAT I MEAN BY THAT. IT'S MORGUES AND UNDER-TAKERS' WORKROOMS AND SUCH. THE CHILL. THE ODORS. THE EERIE CALM.

THE FEELING THAT LIFE HAS NO BUSINESS HERE.

I'M BEING SILLY, I KNOW, BUT THERE YOU ARE.

BUT THEN...IN THE MIDST OF MY UNEASE...

WELL...ERR...WHEN I ***FIRST*** ENCOUNTERED HIM...WE FOUGHT, OBVIOUSLY, AND I WOUNDED HIM... DREW BLOOD...AND MADE A POINT OF KEEPING IT FOR MY COLLECTION.

"OTHER SET-TOS FOLLOWED, ***UNTIL*** ONE TIME...IN '44 TO BE EXACT...WHEN I WAS ***CERTAIN*** HE'D PERISHED BY MOLTEN METAL AND THAT THE CITY AND I WERE FINALLY DONE WITH HIM.

"BUT NO.

HE REAPPEARED SUBSEQUENTLY NOT LONG AFTER.

"AND AGAIN.

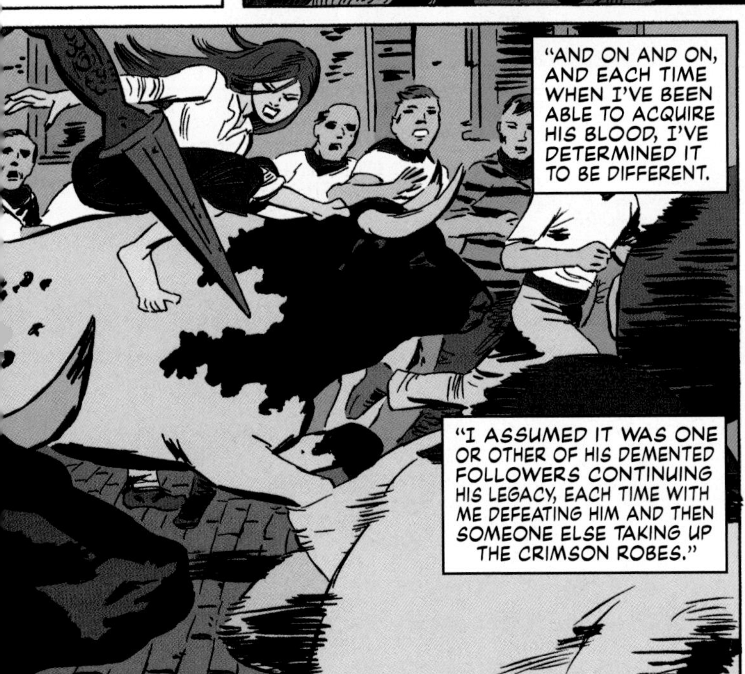
"AND ON AND ON, AND EACH TIME WHEN I'VE BEEN ABLE TO ACQUIRE HIS BLOOD, I'VE DETERMINED IT TO BE DIFFERENT.
"I ASSUMED IT WAS ONE OR OTHER OF HIS DEMENTED FOLLOWERS CONTINUING HIS LEGACY, EACH TIME WITH ME DEFEATING HIM AND THEN SOMEONE ELSE TAKING UP THE CRIMSON ROBES."

UNTIL THE TIME BEFORE THIS ONE. LATE LAST YEAR. BLOOD WAS DRAWN THEN TOO, WHICH I LATER TESTED TO LEARN...
...THIS IS THE ORIGINAL INQUISITOR RETURNED.

SO AFTER HIS MOLTEN "DEATH" HE RESTED, REPAIRED HIMSELF PRESUMABLY, HEALED, AND ALL THE WHILE HAD OTHERS GO OUT IN HIS STEAD.
I AGREE IT CERTAINLY LOOKS THAT WAY, EXCEPT...

...FOR THE ORIGINAL INQUISITOR TO BE ALIVE, HE'D HAVE TO BE CLOSE TO A HUNDRED YEARS OLD. WE SHARE LONGEVITY, YOU AND I, BUT THE INQUISITOR IS A NORMAL MAN... "WAS," I SHOULD SAY.

BUT THAT WAS A MISSTEP ON MY PART. I KNOW WHAT THE LOCATIONS' SIGNIFICANCE IS NOW. THEY'RE ALL SITES WHERE THE INQUISITOR HAD MET DEFEAT IN THE PAST...WITHIN THE CITY, ANYWAY.
YOU'RE RIGHT, OF COURSE. ALL EXCEPT IN SANT MARTI DISTRICT. I DON'T RECALL FIGHTING HIM THERE.

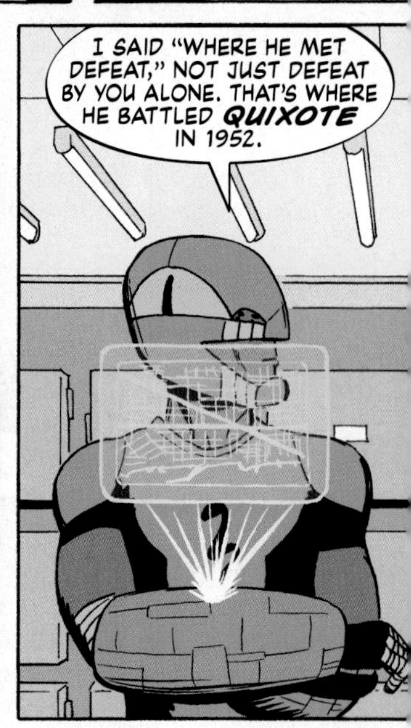
I SAID "WHERE HE MET DEFEAT," NOT JUST DEFEAT BY YOU ALONE. THAT'S WHERE HE BATTLED QUIXOTE IN 1952.

WHAT? YOU VANISHED?
LONG STORY. ANYWAY, MONTPELLIER, WHAT DOES THIS MEAN IN TERMS OF THOSE SUICIDES?
UPON REFLECTION, I STILL THINK THEY ARE WHAT I SAID THEY WERE BEFORE: DARK-BAPTISMS.

AND I'VE A QUESTION FOR YOU, MONTPELLIER. EARLIER WHEN YOU QUESTIONED THAT POLICEMAN, YOU SEEMED CERTAIN THAT THERE WERE FIVE DEAD ACOLYTES, NOT FOUR--WHY WAS THAT?
TO A CATHOLIC, SUICIDE IS A MORTAL SIN. FOR THESE FOLLOWERS OF THE INQUISITOR TO TAKE THEIR LIVES, THERE MUST BE SOMETHING AT STAKE THAT WOULD MAKE IT WORTH ETERNAL DAMNATION.
I SUSPECTED SOME KIND OF RITE. SATANIC, I KNOW, HARDLY "GODLY"... BUT FIVE ACOLYTES, THEIR DEATHS "BAPTIZING" THOSE DIFFERENT LOCATIONS, MAKING THE SHAPE OF A PENTAGRAM WOULD AT LEAST MAKE SOME KIND OF SENSE.

QUIXOTE? LIKE DON QUIXOTE?

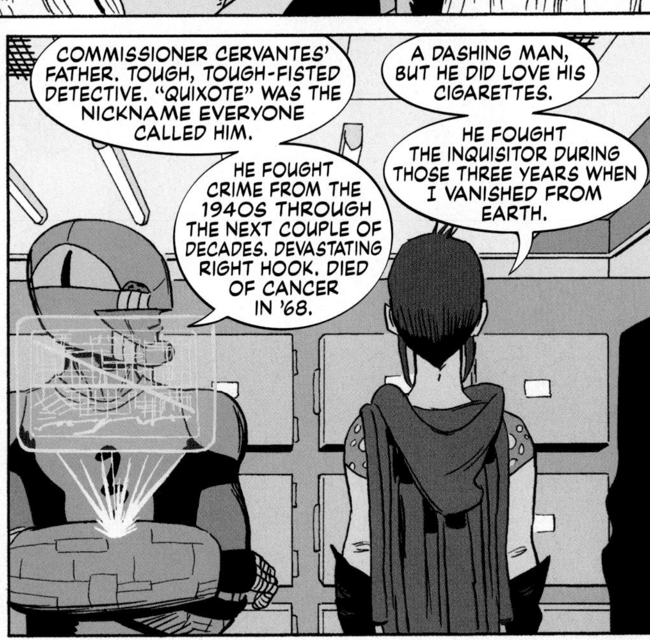

COMMISSIONER CERVANTES' FATHER. TOUGH, TOUGH-FISTED DETECTIVE. "QUIXOTE" WAS THE NICKNAME EVERYONE CALLED HIM.
HE FOUGHT CRIME FROM THE 1940S THROUGH THE NEXT COUPLE OF DECADES. DEVASTATING RIGHT HOOK. DIED OF CANCER IN '68.
A DASHING MAN, BUT HE DID LOVE HIS CIGARETTES.
HE FOUGHT THE INQUISITOR DURING THOSE THREE YEARS WHEN I VANISHED FROM EARTH.

YOU KNOW, LOOKING AT THAT LIST, THERE'S ONE LOCATION MISSING FROM WHEN THE INQUISITOR--AN INQUISITOR ANYWAY--CROSSED SWORDS WITH ME.
YOU'RE SURE?
OF COURSE, FATHER. NOT THE LEAST BECAUSE...

"...THE PLACE IS SO MEMORABLE."

BRRR--I'M SHIVERING THOUGH IT'S WARM TONIGHT. THIS WAITING.
RELAX. **GOD** WILL DELIVER US.
YES, YES, BUT **EVEN** HIS HOLINESS IS DISQUIETED AND UNHAPPY. HE EXPECTED AN ATTACK BY NOW, AND I **HAVE** TO SAY I AGREE.
INDEED? **UNHAPPY,** YOU SAY...?

...THEN LET'S CHEER HIM UP, SHALL WE?

GO, MY LADY! FIND THE INQUISITOR. THE SHADE AND I CAN HANDLE THE REST OF THE ACOLYTE DEFENSES OUT HERE.
I DO SO LOVE BEING BOSSED AROUND, BUT MONTPELLIER DOES HAVE A POINT. GO ON, MY DEAR, DON'T BE TARDY.

NOW...

...YOU HAVE TO UNDERSTAND I FULLY INTENDED TO BE A SUPPORTING PLAYER HERE.
THIS **IS** LA SANGRE'S DRAMA. REMEMBER, THE ONLY REASON I'D TRAVELED TO BARCELONA WAS IN ORDER TO COLLECT A SAMPLE OF MY BLOOD.
NOTHING MORE.
AND HONESTLY, SO FAR, WHAT HAVE I **ACTUALLY** CONTRIBUTED TO THINGS...

...SAVE A COUPLE OF PITHY REMARKS? (AND EVEN IN THAT REGARD I'VE BEEN PITHIER.)
SO FIGHTING OUTLYING DEFENSES WHILE LA SANGRE SAVES THE NIGHT AND THE CITY SEEMS PAR FOR THE COURSE.
I CAN HANDLE THE REST OF THEM. GO, SHADE! YOU TOO! BE WITH OUR LADY!
ODD HOW SUDDENLY THINGS CAN CHANGE ON A CÉNTIMO.

AS TO THE SCENE WHICH GREETED MY ARRIVAL BELOW...WHAT INDEED HAD TRANSPIRED...I CONFESS TO NOT COMPLETELY UNDERSTANDING IT ALL.

--AND GIVE YOU THE SATISFACTION THAT I TURNED MY BACK FROM GOD'S GRACE? ***NEVER!***

NO, I HAVE A ***BETTER*** PLAN...

...I'LL ***STOP*** YOU. I'LL ***SAVE*** THE CITY...

"...SAVE THESE POOR ***INNOCENTS*** YOU HAVE TRAPPED HERE, TOO..."

...AND I'LL RID THE WORLD OF YOUR BLIGHT FOREVER.
YOU CARE ABOUT THIS SCUM? YOU HONESTLY CARE? INNOCENTS, YOU CALL THEM? INNOCENTS?! SINNERS ALL!

LOOK AT THEM--NOTHING BUT UNCTUOUS SODOMITES AND VAIN, PAMPERED WHORES.

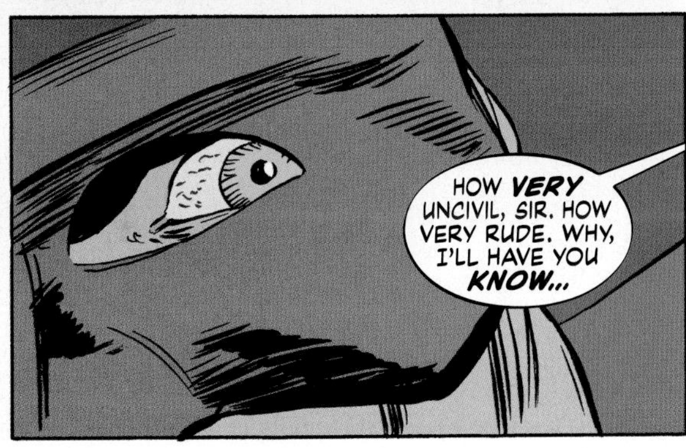
HOW VERY UNCIVIL, SIR. HOW VERY RUDE. WHY, I'LL HAVE YOU KNOW...

...IN **PERHAPS** THE MOST SPECTACULAR DISPLAY OF MY POWERS IN **ALL** OF MY ERRANT EXISTENCE.

LICITADO
HARRIS

The Shade #7 variant cover art by Javier Pulido

I'M SURE I CAN SPEAK FOR LA SANGRE...

...MONTPELLIER TOO, FOR THAT MATTER...

...AND MYSELF, OF COURSE...
...WHEN I SAY THAT ALACRITIES SUCH AS THIS--US AND OUR ENEMIES FIGHTING AT THE CLIMAX OF THIS OR THAT MIS-ADVENTURE--IN ACTUAL TIME THEY TAKE SECONDS... A FEW MINUTES AT MOST, AND YET...
...HOW, IN THE THICK OF EVERY-THING, THOSE MINUTES AND MOMENTS AND SECONDS...

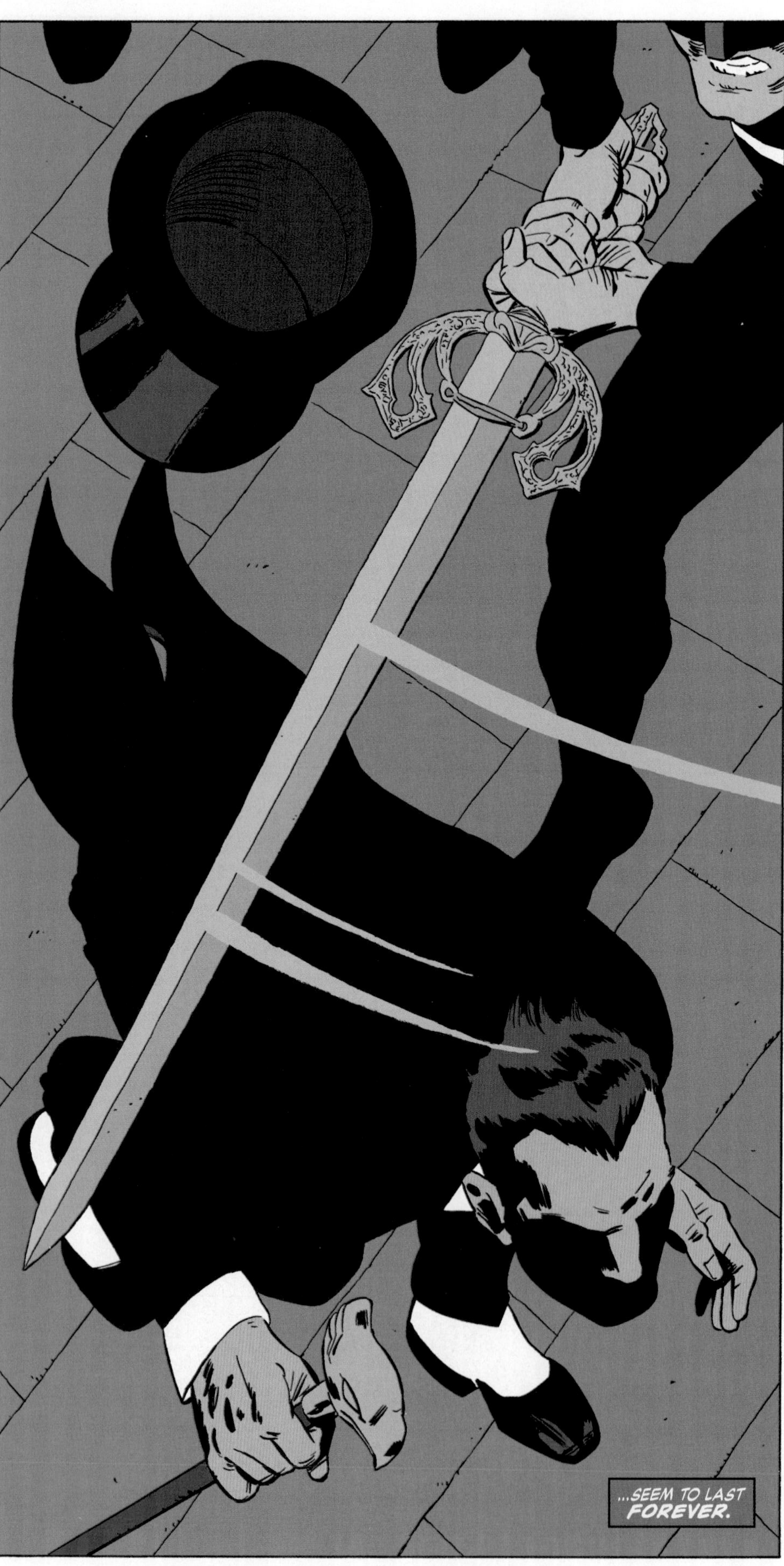

ASCENSIÓN

JAMES ROBINSON
writer

JAVIER PULIDO
artist

HILARY SYCAMORE
colorist

TODD KLEIN
letterer

TONY HARRIS
cover artist

IT'S ALSO NOT WITHOUT A PEPPERING OF IRONY THAT THESE SECONDS PASSING SHOULD BE SO PRECIOUS TO LA SANGRE AND MYSELF, IMMORTALS BOTH OF US.
BUT MUCH IS AT STAKE THIS NIGHT.
FOR LA SANGRE.

FOR HER CITY, BARCELONA.
FOR ITS LANDMARK AND JEWEL, THE SAGRADA FAMÍLIA.

NOT TO MENTION THE FASHION-FORWARD HOSTAGES THE INQUISITOR HOLDS IN SAID BASILICA.

I WAS UNAWARE OF MUCH OF THIS, HOWEVER, HAVING COME UPON THE SPECTACLE LATE, AFTER THE INQUISITOR HAD CONCEDED THE DETAILS OF HIS MACHINATION TO LA SANGRE SOME SEVERAL FEW MINUTES BEFORE I APPEARED HERE WITHIN THE CHURCH.

SOME SEVERAL FEW MINUTES BEFORE...

AHHHH!

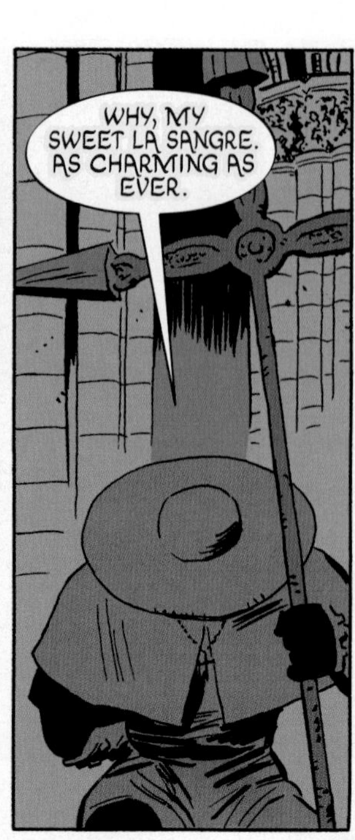

...WHATEVER IN GOD'S NAME THAT IS!

GOD? I DOUBT HE'D APPRECIATE HIS NAME BEING EVOKED FOR WHAT THAT IS.
AS FOR THE HOSTAGES, I'M AFRAID THEY WON'T BE GOING FAR. I NEED THEM--THEIR SOULS AT LEAST--SO I WON'T BE FREEING THEM AS I'D PROMISED.

I MADE A DEAL THERE, A PACT, THAT I RETURN TO EARTH, MY TASK TO CLAIM OTHER SINNERS FOR THE DEVIL'S PLAY.
SO THE "INQUISITORS" THAT I ENCOUNTERED BETWEEN YOUR FIERY EXIT THEN AND YOU HERE NOW WERE ALL IMPOSTORS, AS I SUSPECTED.
IN BODY ALONE... ALL OF THEM ACOLYTES WHO THE DEVIL ALLOWED ME TO POSSESS. IT'S ONLY IN THE LAST LITTLE WHILE I'VE BEEN ALLOWED MY OWN BODY AGAIN.
SO YOU SERVE THE DEVIL NOW, AND YOU DARE CALL ME DEMON? VILE HYPOCRITE!

THAT'S THE BEAUTY OF IT, LA SANGRE--I SERVE SATAN, BUT BY RIDDING THE WORLD OF SINNERS, I SERVE MY LORD IN HEAVEN TOO.
ALL RIGHT THEN, THAT "THING" BEHIND ME? HOW DOES THAT FIT INTO YOUR DELUSION OF GOD'S SERVICE?

THE BEST WAY TO DESCRIBE IT, I'D SAY, IS... WELL...I'D CALL IT A "SOUL BOMB."
A SOUL BOMB? YOU ARE INSANE!
IT NEEDS THE SOULS OF THE HOSTAGES AS KINDLING...SO IT WILL ATTAIN ITS FULL MIGHT AND WORTH.

AT WHICH POINT IT WILL DEVOUR THE SOULS OF EVERYONE IN BARCELONA.

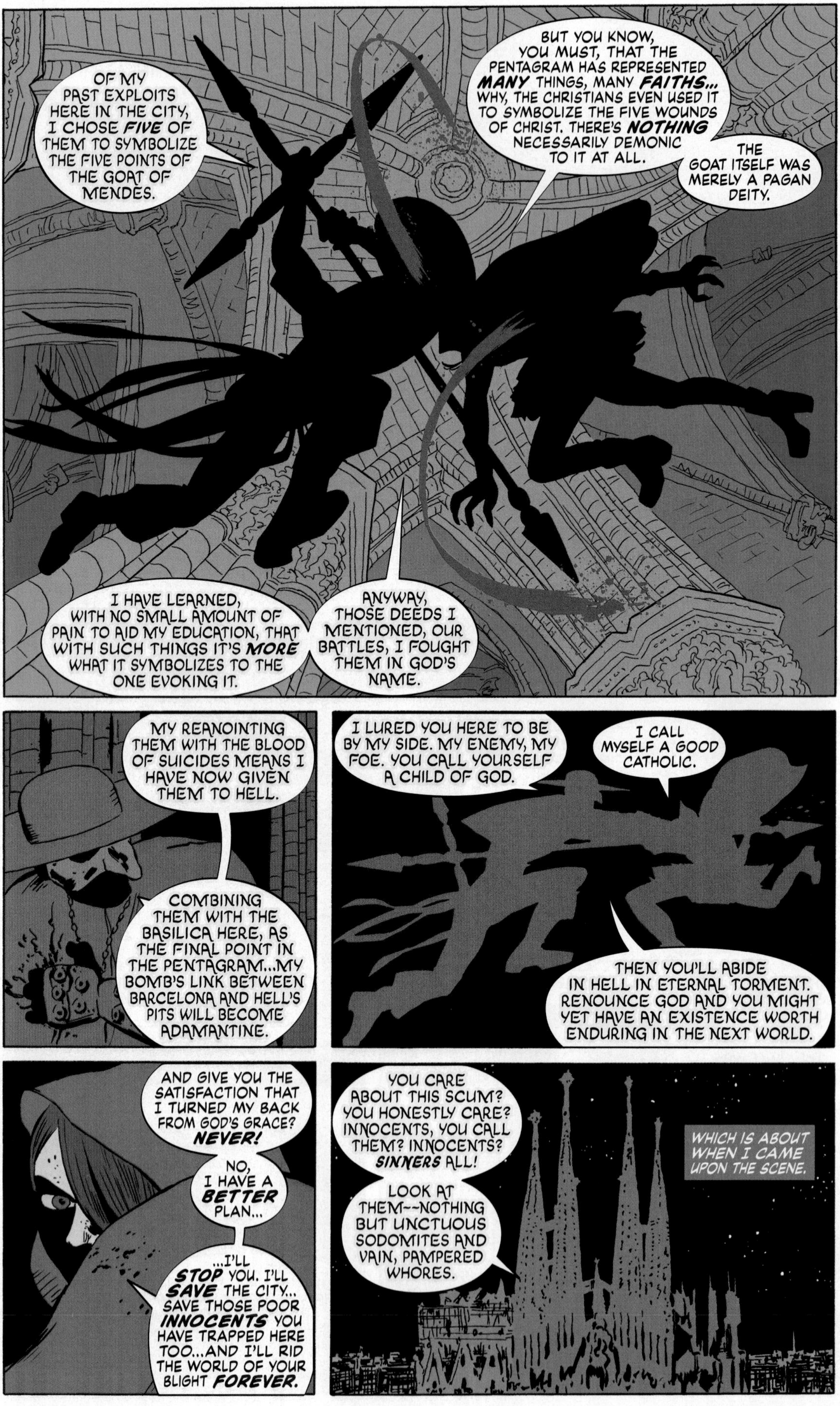

OF MY PAST EXPLOITS HERE IN THE CITY, I CHOSE *FIVE* OF THEM TO SYMBOLIZE THE FIVE POINTS OF THE GOAT OF MENDES.

BUT YOU KNOW, YOU MUST, THAT THE PENTAGRAM HAS REPRESENTED ***MANY*** THINGS, MANY ***FAITHS...*** WHY, THE CHRISTIANS EVEN USED IT TO SYMBOLIZE THE FIVE WOUNDS OF CHRIST. THERE'S ***NOTHING*** NECESSARILY DEMONIC TO IT AT ALL.

THE GOAT ITSELF WAS MERELY A PAGAN DEITY.

I HAVE LEARNED, WITH NO SMALL AMOUNT OF PAIN TO AID MY EDUCATION, THAT WITH SUCH THINGS IT'S ***MORE*** WHAT IT SYMBOLIZES TO THE ONE EVOKING IT.

ANYWAY, THOSE DEEDS I MENTIONED, OUR BATTLES, I FOUGHT THEM IN GOD'S NAME.

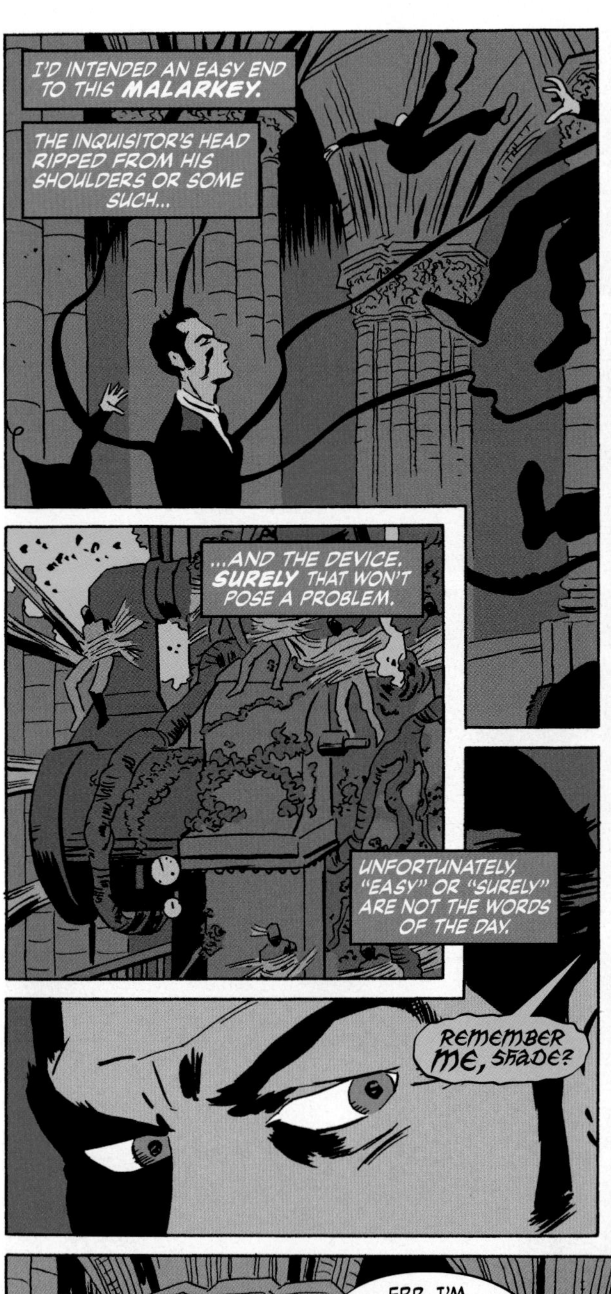
I'D INTENDED AN EASY END TO THIS MALARKEY.
THE INQUISITOR'S HEAD RIPPED FROM HIS SHOULDERS OR SOME SUCH...
...AND THE DEVICE. SURELY THAT WON'T POSE A PROBLEM.
UNFORTUNATELY, "EASY" OR "SURELY" ARE NOT THE WORDS OF THE DAY.
REMEMBER ME, SHADE?

YOU REMEMBER THE LAST TIME WE MET, I BET.

ERR, I'M AFRAID IT MEANT MORE TO YOU THAN I. DRAWING A BLANK.
WE FOUGHT. PARIS. IT WAS A TIME GONE. 1901.
YES, A LONG WHILE. STILL NO BELLS.

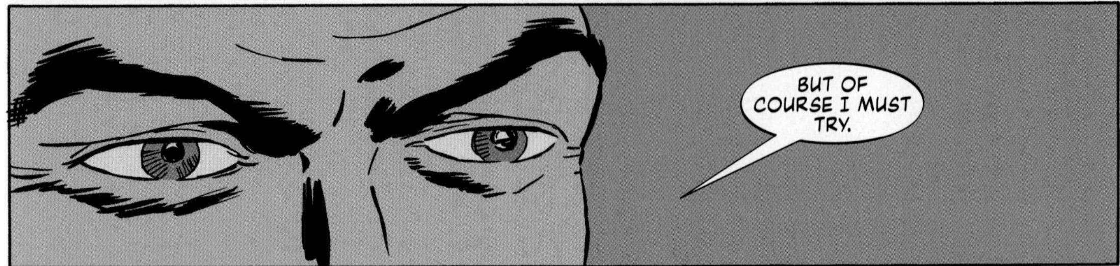

PLEASE. HELP US.

DON'T WORRY, SIR. FOR YOUR ***AUDACIOUS*** CHOICES IN SUIT LININGS ALONE YOU DESERVE TO LIVE.

A QUIP, AS IS MY WONT. BUT STILL, I WONDER...

...IF MY POWERS ARE ENOUGH...IF I HAVE THE MIGHT AND WORTH.

*I HAVE DONE MUCH WITH MY SHADOW, BUT HELL? **...INDEED,** TO BEST HELL WOULD BE A FEAT.*

DO IT, SHADE!

VERY WELL.
FOOL! VAIN FOOL! DIDN'T YOU HEAR ME?
YOU CANNOT WIN!

YES, ABOUT THAT. GOT SOME BAD NEWS FOR YOU, OLD CHAP.
NOW IT BEGINS. **I** BEGIN.
THE SHADOW FLOWS FROM MY FINGERS.

NO!
NHAAHHHH!
THE DARKNESS FLOWS FROM MY ARMS, MY BEING.
BUT ALL AT ONCE, I FEEL SAD.
IT'S THE DEMON, YOU SEE.

SHADE, YOU HAVE TO STOP THE--

AHEAD OF YOU, MY DEAR. WAY AHEAD.
HIS GLEEFUL CITING OF 1901...THE RECOLLECTION OF THAT YEAR FINALLY COMES BACK TO ME.
MY FAMILY. THE REASON I FOUGHT HIM AT THAT TIME AND AGAIN THE REASON I AM HERE NOW, THIS NIGHT.

I THINK OF MY WIFE, REMEMBERING HER FACE THE LAST TIME I SAW HER WHEN I WAS STILL JUST RICHARD SWIFT AND NOT YET THE SHADE. HER EYES WERE BRIGHT THEN, HER CHEEKS AS ROSY AS THE FLOWERS SHE LOVED.

AND HER FACE AGAIN IN 1901, AGED AND BRITTLE, BUT NO LESS LOVELY IN MY EYES.

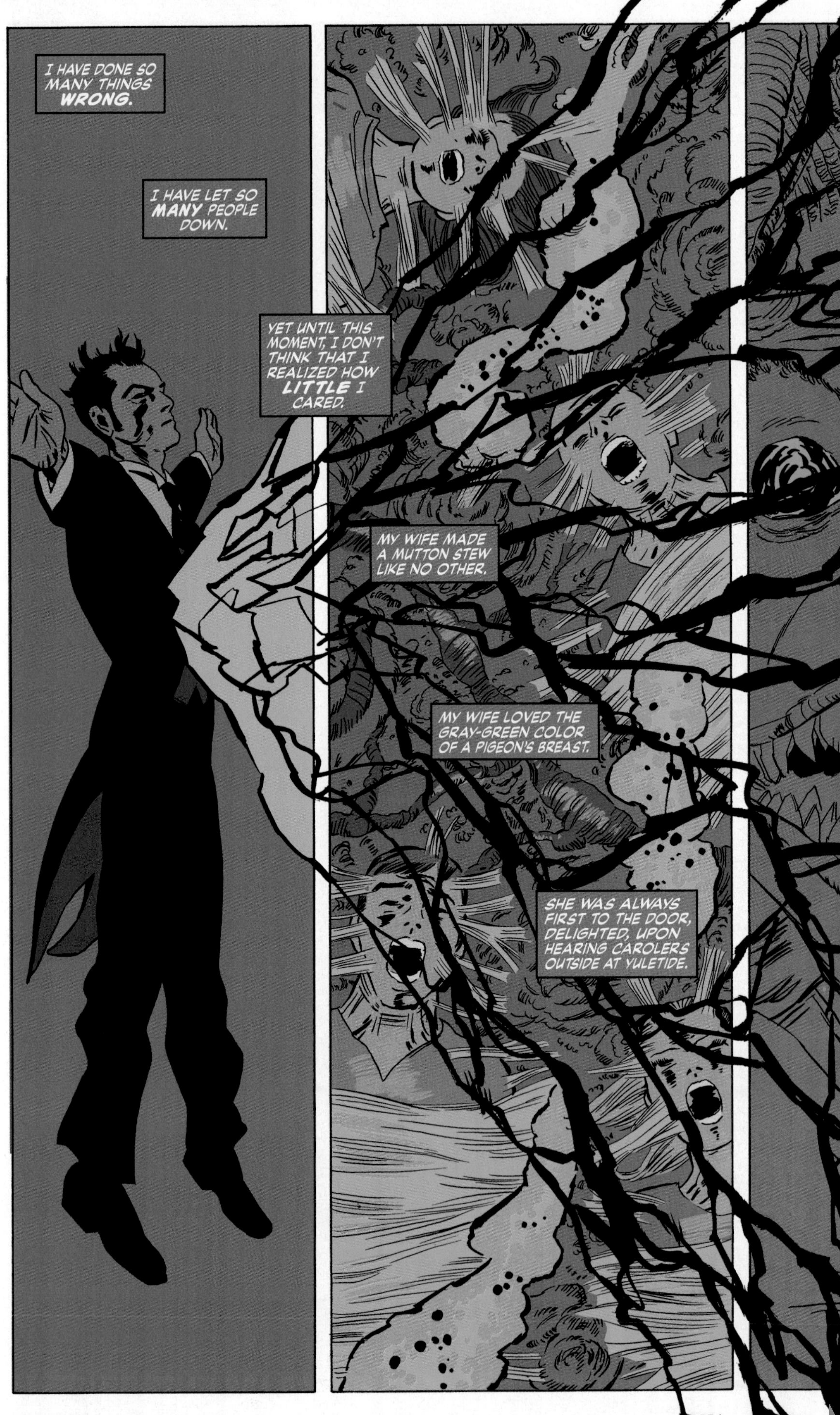
I HAVE DONE SO MANY THINGS WRONG.
I HAVE LET SO MANY PEOPLE DOWN.
YET UNTIL THIS MOMENT, I DON'T THINK THAT I REALIZED HOW LITTLE I CARED.
MY WIFE MADE A MUTTON STEW LIKE NO OTHER.
MY WIFE LOVED THE GRAY-GREEN COLOR OF A PIGEON'S BREAST.
SHE WAS ALWAYS FIRST TO THE DOOR, DELIGHTED, UPON HEARING CAROLERS OUTSIDE AT YULETIDE.

NO! NONO!
HOW? I AM POWER! I AM HELLFIRE AND GLORY!
HOW CAN YOU BE--?
SHE LOVED BREAD AND DRIPPING WITH A HOT CUP OF TEA.
I REALIZE FINALLY... I SEE THAT I WRONGED HER.
DON'T YOU SEE, DEMON?
IT'S ALL A GAMBLE, ALL A GAME. AND QUITE SIMPLY... YOU'VE BEEN OUTPLAYED.
AND SO I AM SAD.
IT WON'T END! NOT THIS WAY! CAN'T LET--

THESE THEN...
...ARE MY THOUGHTS AS I SPIN SHADOW OUTWARDS, ONWARDS, BARELY REGISTERING WHAT I AM DOING OR HOW MUCH.

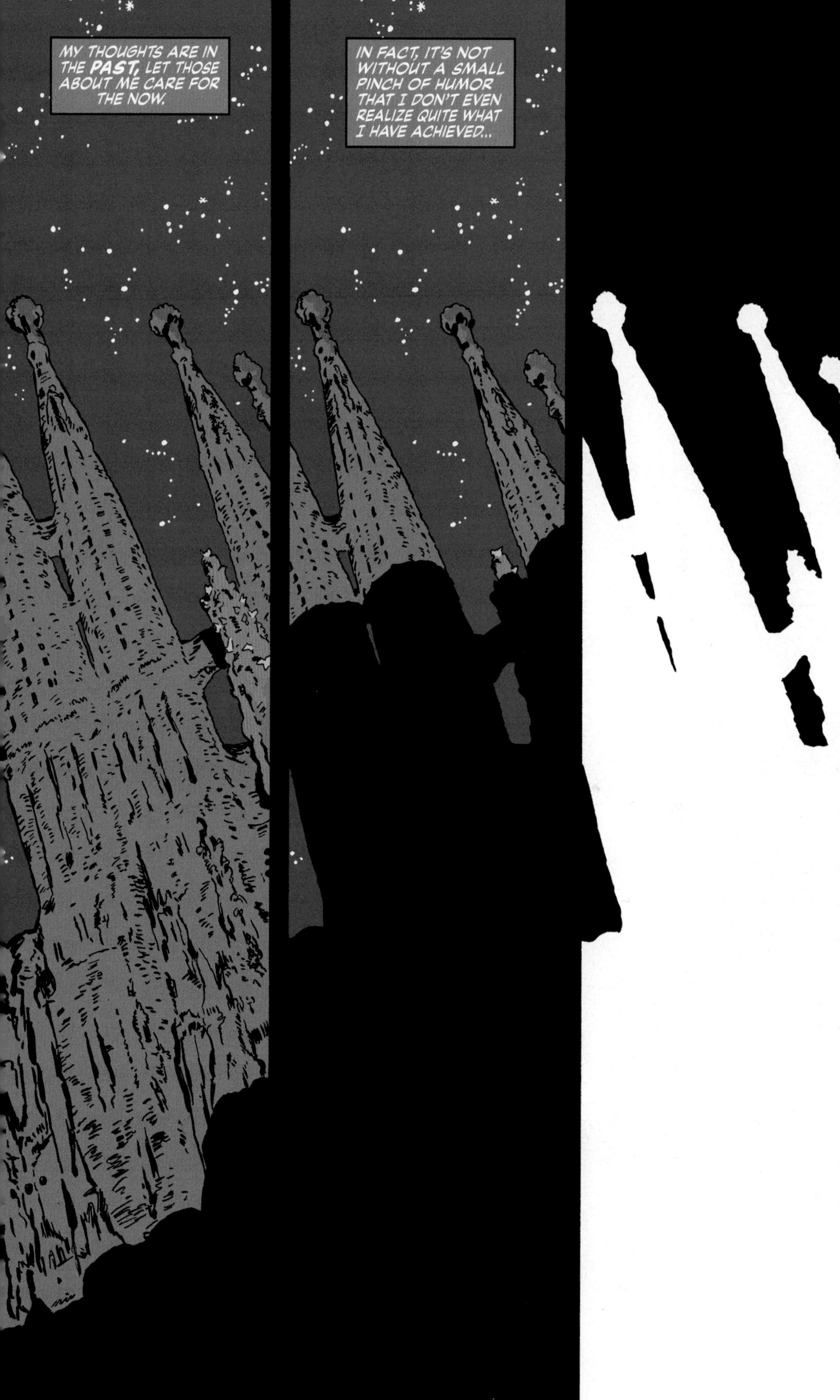
MY THOUGHTS ARE IN THE PAST, LET THOSE ABOUT ME CARE FOR THE NOW.
IN FACT, IT'S NOT WITHOUT A SMALL PINCH OF HUMOR THAT I DON'T EVEN REALIZE QUITE WHAT I HAVE ACHIEVED...

...UNTIL **AFTER**
I AM **DONE!**

LATER.

SO...

...DO YOU THINK THE INQUISITOR ESCAPED OR PERISHED?
ALL I KNOW IS HE SLIPPED FROM MY GRASP BEFORE THE FINAL WAVE OF BLACK-NESS ENGULFED EVERYTHING.
BELIEVE IT OR NOT, IT'S HARD FOR ME TO TELL IF I'VE CONSIGNED SOMEONE TO THE SHADOW REALM UNLESS I SEE THEM GO, AND IN THIS INSTANCE I WAS SOMEWHAT DISTRACTED.

SO HE MAY BE DEAD, LOST IN THE SHADE'S DARKNESS, OR RUNNING FREE AND CLEAR TO PLAN ANEW.
YES.
AND WHICHEVER, WHATEVER THE OUTCOME, I'LL DEAL WITH IT, AS I HAVE THIS FAR.
WHAT'S IMPORTANT IS THE SHADE SENT THE "SOUL BOMB" TO WHEREVER HE "SENDS" THINGS AND HE SAVED EVERYONE.

YES, I DID.

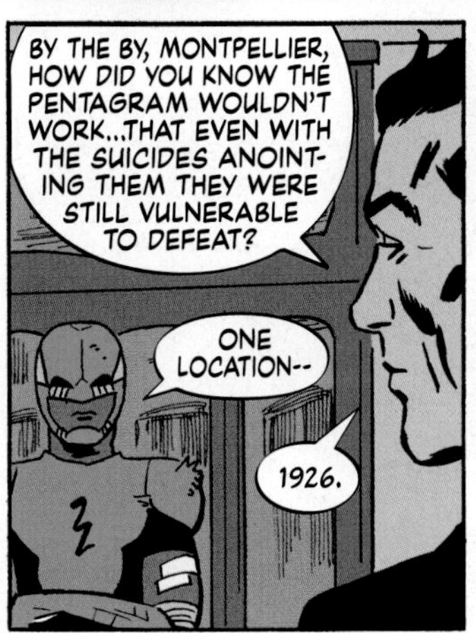

BY THE BY, MONTPELLIER, HOW DID YOU KNOW THE PENTAGRAM WOULDN'T WORK...THAT EVEN WITH THE SUICIDES ANOINT-ING THEM THEY WERE STILL VULNERABLE TO DEFEAT?
ONE LOCATION--
1926.

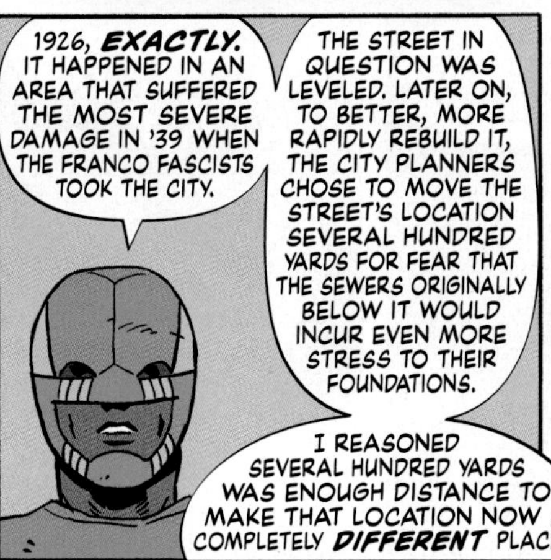

1926, ***EXACTLY.*** IT HAPPENED IN AN AREA THAT SUFFERED THE MOST SEVERE DAMAGE IN '39 WHEN THE FRANCO FASCISTS TOOK THE CITY.
THE STREET IN QUESTION WAS LEVELED. LATER ON, TO BETTER, MORE RAPIDLY REBUILD IT, THE CITY PLANNERS CHOSE TO MOVE THE STREET'S LOCATION SEVERAL HUNDRED YARDS FOR FEAR THAT THE SEWERS ORIGINALLY BELOW IT WOULD INCUR EVEN MORE STRESS TO THEIR FOUNDATIONS.
I REASONED SEVERAL HUNDRED YARDS WAS ENOUGH DISTANCE TO MAKE THAT LOCATION NOW A COMPLETELY ***DIFFERENT*** PLACE...

...SOMETHING A SUICIDAL ACOLYTE MIGHT OVER-LOOK.
HMM.
YOU ***ARE*** A CLEVER FELLOW.

TWO HOURS PASS.
I HAVE SOME BAD NEWS, FATHER...

...I WENT TO MY VAULT WHERE I STORE MY COLLECTION OF BLOOD. I FOUND THE SAMPLE OF YOURS, BUT IT WAS SO OLD THAT IT HAD SPOILED DESPITE MY BEST EFFORTS.
I'M SORRY.

NO MATTER. I HAVE BAD NEWS OF MY OWN. THE PHONE CALL WAS FROM THE DETECTIVE VON HAMMER, WHO INFORMS ME THAT MY GREAT-GRANDSON DARNELL HAS DIED.
THE BLOOD WAS FOR HIM, AND WITH HIS PASSING I'D SAY IT'S BEST SPOILED AND GONE FOR GOOD.

SO WHAT WILL YOU DO?
END WHAT DARNELL BEGAN. ENGLAND. LONDON, ENGLAND, IF I'M TO FIND THE BAD APPLE ON MY FAMILY TREE.

THEN I'LL GO WITH YOU. AFTER ALL YOU'VE DONE, IT'S THE LEAST--

NO. STAY HERE AND BE VIGILANT FOR THE INQUISITOR, WHO MAY YET BE ALIVE--AND SPITTING FURY TOO, IF HE IS, I'LL BET. HE'S CAPABLE OF ANYTHING.

THEN WHEN WILL I SEE YOU AGAIN? YOU ALWAYS GO FOR SO LONG EVERY TIME, AND I MISS YOU ALREADY.
NOT THIS TIME. I'LL COME BACK AS SOON AS MY MYSTERY IS SOLVED, I SWEAR.

VERY WELL. THOUGH IT BREAKS MY HEART TO SAY IT...
...FAREWELL, FATHER. UNTIL THEN.

SOON...
I HAVE DONE SO MANY THINGS WRONG.
I HAVE LET SO MANY PEOPLE DOWN.

...I PROMISE, WE'LL MEET AGAIN...

...MY DAUGHTER.

LONDON.

MY WONDROUS LORD.

I HAVE WORD OF THE SHADE...HE WAS IN SPAIN, SOME SORT OF DRAMA, NOTHING TO DO WITH US THANKFULLY, BUT...
...SINCE THEN HE'S VANISHED, AND I CAN'T THINK OF ANY REASON WHY HE WOULDN'T BE COMING HERE.
A STORM APPROACHES? FINALLY...

...SOMETHING TO ENTERTAIN ME.

METROPOLITAIN

The Shade #8 variant cover art by Jill Thompson & Trish Mulvihill

ABSINTHE.
WHAT A **DELIGHTFUL** NOTION. ABSINTHE IT SHALL BE.

AND PASS THE PIPE, WOULD YOU?
NO, ON SECOND THOUGHT, DON'T BOTHER.

YVETTE, MY LOVELY YVETTE, WOULD YOU BE AN ANGEL AND BRING ME ANOTHER PIPE...?
...NO NEED TO DEPRIVE THIS FELLOW HIS OWN.
AND ABSINTHE FOR THIS YOUNG MAN AND I.

YOU KNOW...
YOU KNOW, I'VE CHANGED MY MIND. DO THEY HAVE SCOTCH HERE, DO YOU THINK?
WHY WOULDN'T THEY?

NOT BEEN IN THE CITY ALL THAT LONG. FEW MONTHS... FROM LONDON--
YES, I HEAR YOUR ACCENT.
--AND I'M NOT SURE WHAT'S WHAT YET. HERE. WHAT THEY HAVE...LOT OF WINE AND COGNAC, OBVIOUSLY. SCOTCH, THOUGH?

MY DEAR FELLOW, THIS IS PARIS...

TIMES PAST: 1901
FAMILY TIES PART II
JAMES ROBINSON writer
JILL THOMPSON artist
TRISH MULVIHILL colorist
TODD KLEIN letterer
TONY HARRIS cover artist
...AND PARIS HAS EVERYTHING A MAN COULD WANT.
1901 was a good year for me.
I'd accepted my powers by then, fully, truly.
I had been evil, at least as defined by mankind's labels...

...murderous even at times, I admit.

SO, YOUNG MAN, DO YOU HAVE A NAME?

EH? WHAT?

But I had been kind, too. My moods and mores since "rebirth" capricious at best.

I was "The Shade" by then. My sobriquet given to me as a joke by Oscar, but readily...no, greedily claimed so I might all the more distance myself from the sad thing I now regarded my prior humanity to be.

YOUR NAME.

OH, OF COURSE. SORRY, I'M DRIFTING SO.

St. Dubris, some 50 miles south of Paris. At that moment.
WHY SO GLUM, MAYOR ROUSSEAU? I'D HAVE THOUGHT YOU'D BE DELIGHTED.

I MEAN, LOOK AT THE HISTORY OF YOUR PEOPLE. THE FRENCH. CONSTANTLY AT WAR WITH ENGLAND. CONSTANTLY AT WAR WITH YOURSELVES, FOR THAT MATTER.
THE FRENCH REVOLUTION--WHAT WAS THAT EXACTLY? THE POPULACE RISING UP AGAINST ITS UNCARING ROYALTY?

OR SIMPLY ONE MORE EXCUSE TO LET THE BLOOD FLOW?

NEVER MIND ALL THOSE WHO CLIMBED THE STEPS TO THE GUILLOTINE, WHAT ABOUT THE SEPTEMBER MASSACRES? WHEN WAS THAT, 1793? NO, '92, THAT'S RIGHT. GHASTLY BEYOND ANYTHING--AND THIS IS ME TALKING.
OR 1572. MASSACRE DE LA SAINT-BARTHÉLEMY. CLOSE TO 27,000 HUGUENOTS DEAD.

PLEASE. DON'T KILL ME.

LET ME FINISH, PLEASE. MY POINT...
AS I SAID, AFTER ALL THE EFFORT I WENT TO, I'M A LITTLE HURT. YOU'RE ALL "WOE IS ME," WHEN I'D HAVE THOUGHT YOU'D BE HAPPY.
AFTER ALL...

"...DON'T THE FRENCH LOVE IT WHEN THEIR GUTTERS RUN RED WITH ***BLOOD?***"

THE CHILDREN. ALL THE CHILDREN OF THE TOWN.
DELICIOUS.
MY WIFE.

DID YOU KNOW THAT ANYONE KILLED BY SUCH AS I...NO MATTER HOW CHASTE, HOW CHARMING THEIR LIVES MAY HAVE BEEN...
...THEIR SOULS GO TO MY REALM, NOT THE HALLS OF CHOIRS AND LIGHT?
HELL.

CERTAINLY ONE WORD FOR IT. YOUR WIFE IS ALREADY THERE.
MY BROTHERS ALL TAKE TURNS WITH HER, TWO AT A TIME.

BARBED AND SCALY THEY MAY BE-- AND SCREAMS? OH, HOW YOUR WIFE CRIES...YET IN HER HEART I'M SURE SHE LIKES IT BETTER THAN THE PLACID, FLACCID OFFERINGS OF HER SILLY HUSBAND.
AND BY THAT I MEAN YOU, MAYOR, OF COURSE.

IF I AM TO DIE, **HURRY UP** AND BE ON YOUR WAY.

NO. I LIKE TO LEAVE **ONE** BEHIND. LUCKY YOU.
GOOD DAY, SIR...

...IT'S BEEN A PLEASURE.

Paris.
SO HOW DO WE FEEL NOW?
REVIVED, I HOPE.
HONESTLY, I FEEL LIKE I'VE BEEN TRAMPLED BY SHIRE HORSES. I'M GLAD YOU CONVINCED ME TO LEAVE THAT PLACE.
YES, "LE JARDIN CRAMOISI" TRULY IS A GARDEN OF EARTHLY PLEASURES...
...BUT I'VE SEEN WEAKER MEN THAN WE WITHER AWAY TO NOTHING THERE.
MODERATION IN ALL THINGS--INCLUDING MODERATION.
FUNNY.
AND ALAS, NOT MINE OWN. A FRIEND'S QUIP REWORDED.
SO, YOUNG ALBERT CALDECOTT, WHAT BRINGS YOU TO PARIS?
A WANDERING HEART. AND MY FATHER TELLING ME NEVER TO SHOW MY FACE AGAIN. THAT MIGHT HAVE SOMETHING TO DO WITH IT.
WELL, I KNOW SO EXTREME A THING IS NEVER VOICED WITHOUT REASON. IS IT THE PIPE? DOES IT HOLD YOU TIGHTER THAN I THOUGHT? OR SOME OTHER VICE--GAMBLING? THE BOTTLE? WOMEN? BOYS?

ALL OF THEM AT ONE TIME OR ANOTHER. THE THING... THE FINAL STRAW...WAS MY INVOLVEMENT WITH A SOCIETY.
THE HERMETIC ORDER OF THE GOLDEN DAWN.
AH. CROWLEY.

YOU KNOW OF HIM? DO YOU HAVE MUCH BROOK WITH MAGIC?
DO I BELIEVE? I THINK FOR ANY TRUE MAGE OUT THERE--AND THEY ARE OUT THERE--THERE ARE ALSO MANY DILETTANTES AND IDLERS WHO USE THE THEATER OF IT ALL AS AN EXCUSE TO DRESS UP IN LONG ROBES AND ENJOY UNBRIDLED FORNICATION.
CROWLEY, TO MY MIND, WALKS A LINE SOMEWHERE BETWEEN THE TWO.

WELL, IT ISN'T CROWLEY, ANYWAY.
"ANYWAY"--WHAT? I'M NOT FOLLOWING YOU.
THE FELLOW WHO... YOU KNOW...WHY I'M HERE.

OTTO HADDON WAS PART OF THE ORDER... WHICH BY THE END OF '98 WAS RAPIDLY BREAKING UP. I JOINED JUST LONG ENOUGH TO MEET HADDON AND... WELL...
YOU BECAME INVOLVED.
IF THE NOTION DOESN'T DISGUST YOU TO HEAR, LET ME SAY IT: I LOVED HIM.

RELAX, IT TAKES A GOOD DEAL TO MAKE ME BLUSH. PRAY CONTINUE.
HE WAS A MAGICIAN. MY GOD, THE THINGS HE KNEW... COULD DO. I FOLLOWED HIM HERE, TO PARIS, AGAINST MY FATHER'S WISHES.

I WATCHED OTTO...HELPED HIM AT TIMES, TOO...USE MORE AND MORE EXTREME FORMS OF ARCANISM. ANIMAL SACRIFICE, INCANTATIONS IN FORGOTTEN LANGUAGES--ALL MANNER.
UNTIL HE CREATED A HOMUNCULUS.

HOMUNCULUS.
A DEMONIC SERVANT.
OH, I KNOW WHAT ONE IS, IT'S JUST NOT A WORD ONE *EXPECTS* TO HEAR THAT OFTEN.

THE THING IS, IT SOUNDS BENIGN...SERVILE... BUT IT'S ACTUALLY STILL A PRETTY STRONG MINOR DEMON--
--AND CONTROL OVER IT IS DETERMINED BY THE INVOKER'S RESOLVE. OTTO LOVED ME, HE LOVED MAGIC...
...BUT HE ALSO HAD QUITE AN AFFECTION FOR LAUDANUM. IT WEAKENED HIS WILL, AND--
I DON'T KNOW WHY I'M BEING SO CANDID. I'VE ONLY JUST MET YOU.

PERHAPS IT'S JUST THAT I HAVE ONE OF THOSE FACES. SO WHAT HAPPENED NEXT? GO ON!
THE DEMON POSSESSED OTTO. *MY* OTTO. ATE HIS SOUL.

NOW IN OTTO'S FORM IT TRAVELS THE COUNTRY COMMITTING ACTS OF ***MURDEROUS DEPRAVITY.***
AND THEN IT RETURNS TO ME.
WHY YOU?

I WAS THERE AT ITS SUMMONING. I'M *LINKED* TO IT SOMEHOW.
I'M FORCED TO DO THINGS I'D RATHER NOT SPEAK OF, AND ALL THE WHILE WITH HIM TELLING ME OF HIS TERRIBLE DEEDS...WHISPERING THEM INTO MY EAR AS A LOVER MIGHT UTTER ADORATIONS.

HE'S--
IT'S GONE AT THE MOMENT, BUT WILL **SURELY** RETURN. THAT'S WHY, IN THIS LULL, YOU FOUND ME SEEKING SOLACE IN THE POPPY.
YOU'VE TRIED RUNNING, I SUPPOSE?
TRIED. FOUND. BROUGHT BACK TO THE CITY. AND TOLD THAT, IF I RAN AGAIN, MY SOUL WOULD FOLLOW OTTO'S.

TELL ME ABOUT YOUR FAMILY, ALBERT.

NOT MUCH TO TELL. THEY'RE WEALTHY AND WANT **NOTHING** TO DO WITH THEIR WASTREL, SODOMITE OFFSPRING.

WEALTHY HOW SO?
IT WAS MY GRANDMOTHER, **ELIZABETH.**

BESSY.

YES, THAT WAS THE NAME MY GRANDFATHER CALLED HER BEFORE HE DESERTED HER... LONG AGO THIS WAS. HOW DID YOU KNOW?
ERR. UM. GO ON. YOUR GRAND-MOTHER?

WELL, UPON MY GRANDMOTHER BEING ABANDONED, SHE FOUND WORK AT A DISPENSING CHEMIST'S, LEARNING CHEMISTRY AS SHE WENT.
SHE SAVED, SCRIMPED, AND AFTER A TIME SHE BOUGHT THE SHOP UPON HER EMPLOYER'S RETIREMENT.

ONE SHOP BECAME MANY AND, DESPITE BEING A WOMAN IN WHAT WE CAN ALL AGREE IS A MAN'S SOCIETY, SHE CREATED A SMALL EMPIRE FOR HERSELF.
AS SHE GREW OLDER, HER SON-IN-LAW--MY FATHER--THEN TOOK IT ON AND ADDED OTHER BUSINESSES... FACTORIES AND SUCH, FORMING WHAT'S SHAPING INTO AN EVEN BIGGER ENTERPRISE.
AND THERE WE ARE.

IT WOULD VERY MUCH PLEASE ME, ALBERT, IF I COULD TRANSFORM YOU FROM WASTREL TO PRODIGAL SCION IN THE EYES OF YOUR FAMILY.
HONESTLY, I WOULD LIKE TO SEE MY DEAR OLD GRANNY AGAIN.

WAIT. SHE'S ALIVE?
VERY OLD, BUT HANGING ON. WALKING, EVEN. DOESN'T NEED A CANE, EXCEPT UPON VERY COLD DAYS.

ALL THE MORE REASON THIS DEMON SHOULD BE DEALT WITH AND I GET YOU ON THE CHANNEL FERRY BACK HOME TO HER.
WHAT MUST I DO?

TRUST ME.

...COME TO ME. **NOW.** TO **ME.**
COME HEAR MY **TALES.**
Of course Albert was by then relocated to my apartment.
TEMPTING...

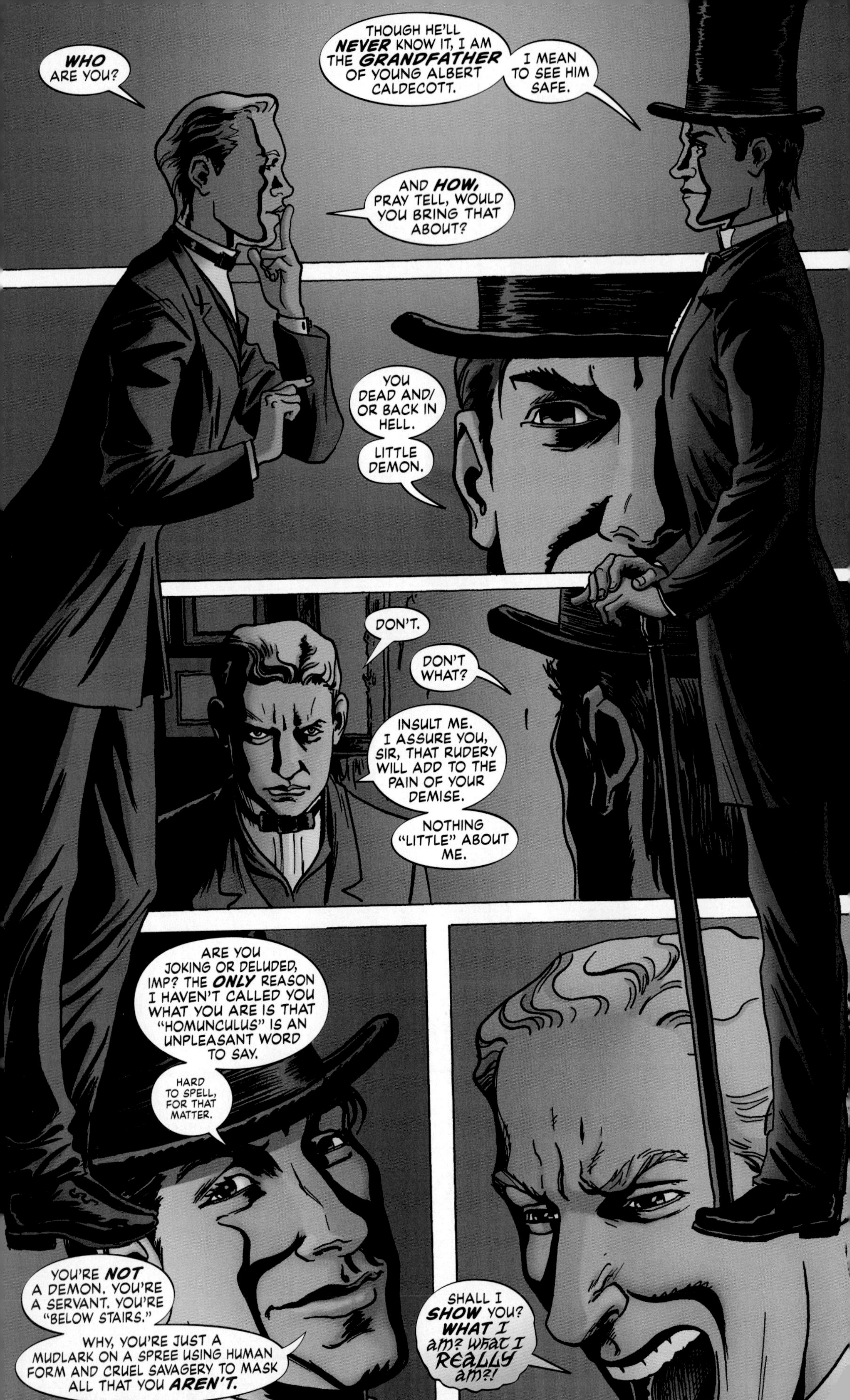
WHO ARE YOU?
THOUGH HE'LL NEVER KNOW IT, I AM THE GRANDFATHER OF YOUNG ALBERT CALDECOTT.
I MEAN TO SEE HIM SAFE.
AND HOW, PRAY TELL, WOULD YOU BRING THAT ABOUT?
YOU DEAD AND/ OR BACK IN HELL.
LITTLE DEMON.
DON'T.
DON'T WHAT?
INSULT ME. I ASSURE YOU, SIR, THAT RUDERY WILL ADD TO THE PAIN OF YOUR DEMISE.
NOTHING "LITTLE" ABOUT ME.
ARE YOU JOKING OR DELUDED, IMP? THE ONLY REASON I HAVEN'T CALLED YOU WHAT YOU ARE IS THAT "HOMUNCULUS" IS AN UNPLEASANT WORD TO SAY.
HARD TO SPELL, FOR THAT MATTER.
YOU'RE NOT A DEMON. YOU'RE A SERVANT. YOU'RE "BELOW STAIRS."
WHY, YOU'RE JUST A MUDLARK ON A SPREE USING HUMAN FORM AND CRUEL SAVAGERY TO MASK ALL THAT YOU AREN'T.
SHALL I SHOW YOU? WHAT I am? WHAT I REALLY am?!

am I a SERVANT?!
IS THIS a SERVANT?!
Of course by now I knew the difference between size and power.

How the two so often do *not* go hand in hand.

...feeling churlish and disinclined to coddle the creature...

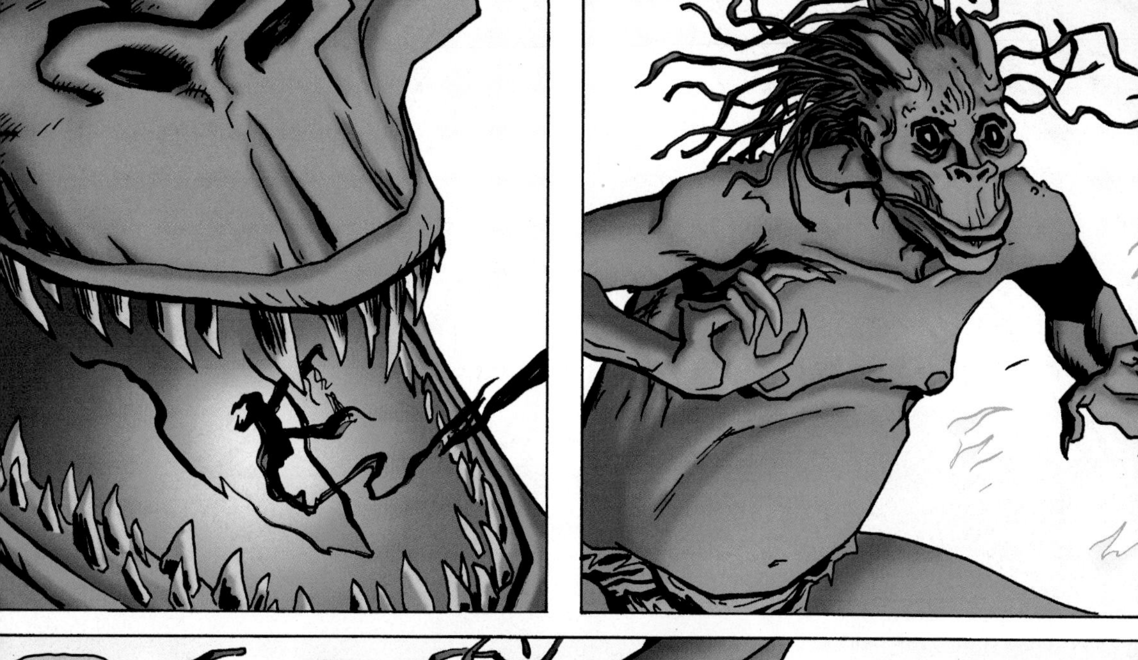

...I decided to prove the point by example.
YES! BACK TO HELL WITH YOU!

A week later. Belgrave Square, London, England.
WHAT SHOULD I SAY?
WHATEVER YOU HAVE TO. EARN THEIR TRUST AND LOVE ANEW.
AND IF YOU TAKE ANY MORE LOVERS MORE SUITED TO PANTS THAN PETTICOATS, FOR HEAVEN'S SAKE, BE DISCREET ABOUT IT.

THERE!...

...MY GRANDMOTHER AWAITS ME. SHE GOT THE CABLE I SENT.
SEE? FOR ONE SO OLD SHE STILL HAS A YOUTHFUL WAY TO HER, WOULDN'T YOU SAY?

INDEED.
SHE'S LOVELY.

COME, LET ME INTRODUCE YOU AT LEAST.
NO.

I'LL WATCH FROM AFAR.
It was something of a reward, I suppose. A gift.
To know my wife had lived such a life (surely a better one than if I'd stayed)...
...and, albeit from a distance, to see her sweetness one final time.
I heard later that in the spring of '04 she died. Did I shed a tear at that time? Hmm.
I don't recall.

HARRIS
HARRIS

The Shade #9 variant cover art by Frazer Irving

I HAD SAID THE THEME OF MY BARCELONA SOJOURN WAS THAT OF "BLOOD."
BUT THAT WAS BARCELONA.
UPON MY RETURN TO LONDON...
...THIS BEING THE BIRTHPLACE OF THE SHADE AND RICHARD SWIFT BOTH, AFTER ALL...
...I'D ASSUMED THAT THE CONCLUSION TO BE MADE... THAT THE OVERRIDING THEME OF THIS--MY ODYSSEY FROM OPAL TO ENGLAND'S CAPITAL--WOULD BE ONE OF "FAMILY."
IT'S ONLY NOW, WALKING STREETS SADLY BEREFT THE MASONRY AND COBBLESTONES OF YORE, AND YET SO FAMILIAR TO MY HEART--THAT I CLEARLY SEE WHAT THIS ENTERPRISE IS TRULY ABOUT.
AS WITH MANY OF MY SINGULAR TRAVAILS, IN THE END IT ALL BOILS DOWN TO ONE FAMILIAR, SIMPLE THING...
...THE PAST.
MEMPHIS, EGYPT, 2681 B.C.
I DON'T KNOW ABOUT YOU...

...BUT *I'M* GETTING *BORED.*

OF LONDON NOW AND EGYPT THEN

JAMES ROBINSON WRITER
FRAZER IRVING ARTIST & COLORIST
TODD KLEIN LETTERER
TONY HARRIS COVER ARTIST

"SO, MILES, TELL ME..."
...HOW WAS NIGERIA?
NIGERIA? DUSTY.
YES, THAT WOULD BE THE WORD I'D USE TO DESCRIBE THE PLACE. WHY, YOU COULD GIVE EVERYONE IN LAGOS THEIR OWN VACUUM CLEANER AND THE CITY WOULD STILL TURN WHITE LINEN TO GRAY IN MINUTES.
I'D HAVE WORN MY TRACKSUIT, BUT I ALWAYS THINK THAT MAKES ONE LOOK LIKE A RUSSIAN GANGSTER, DON'T YOU AGREE?
YOU HAVE A POINT. STILL, JAHSWILL ENEBELI, HE'S...?
AT ONE WITH THE DODOS, OLD CHUM. OH, DO RELAX, DUDLEY.
WE'RE FREE AND CLEAR NOW TO DRILL FOR OIL UP AND DOWN THEIR COASTLINE WITHOUT FEAR OF ENEBELI'S GETTING ELECTED AND ALL HIS TALK OF ECOLOGICAL PRESERVATION RILING THE POPULACE.
OH, AND I HAD THE GUNMEN MAKE IT LOOK LIKE A ROBBERY-MURDER SO WE NEEDN'T WORRY ABOUT ANY "MARTYR" NONSENSE EITHER.
CIGARETTE?
TRYING TO QUIT--THEY'LL KILL YOU, YOU KNOW.
FAIR ENOUGH. ANYWAY, IF IT'S QUESTION TIME...AFGHANISTAN?
EVERYTHING WE'D HOPED FOR.
THE WEAPONS AND EXPLOSIVES WERE DELIVERED TO THE INSURGENTS AS PER. THEY IN TURN HAVE OPENED THEIR POPPY FIELDS TO OUR COLLEAGUES IN MARSEILLES. WHO IN TURN HAVE OUR SHOWPIECE IN PARIS COMING TOGETHER NICELY.

AS PER.
AS PER.
COME, THE OTHERS ARE WAITING FOR US.
ABSOLUTELY. HATE TO APPEAR THOUGHTLESS. HAVE TO MAKE THIS QUICK, ANYWAY--I'M DUE AT DOWNING STREET WITHIN THE HOUR. LUNCH WITH THE P.M.-- HE WANTS MY ADVICE ON IRELAND.
IRELAND? EASY, NUKE THE WHOLE BLOODY PLACE. BEST THING.
HA! IF ONLY IT WERE THAT SIMPLE. UNFORTUNATELY, AS THIS CONCERNS THE DAIRY WORKERS ON STRIKE THERE, I'VE THE FISCAL INTERESTS OF SOME IMPORTANT MEN TO CONSIDER, SO I DOUBT I CAN BE SO--
--ERR... WHAT IS THE WORD I'M LOOKING FOR?...UM...NOT BLOODTHIRSTY EXACTLY... ERR--
LORD CALDECOTT, SIR, EXCUSE THE PUN, BUT I BELIEVE THE WORD THAT'S ELUDING YOU IS "CUTTHROAT."
INDEED, THACKERY, INDEED IT IS.
NOW, LET'S MAKE THIS SNAPPY...
PLEASE, NO...

...CAN'T KEEP THE P.M. WAITING.

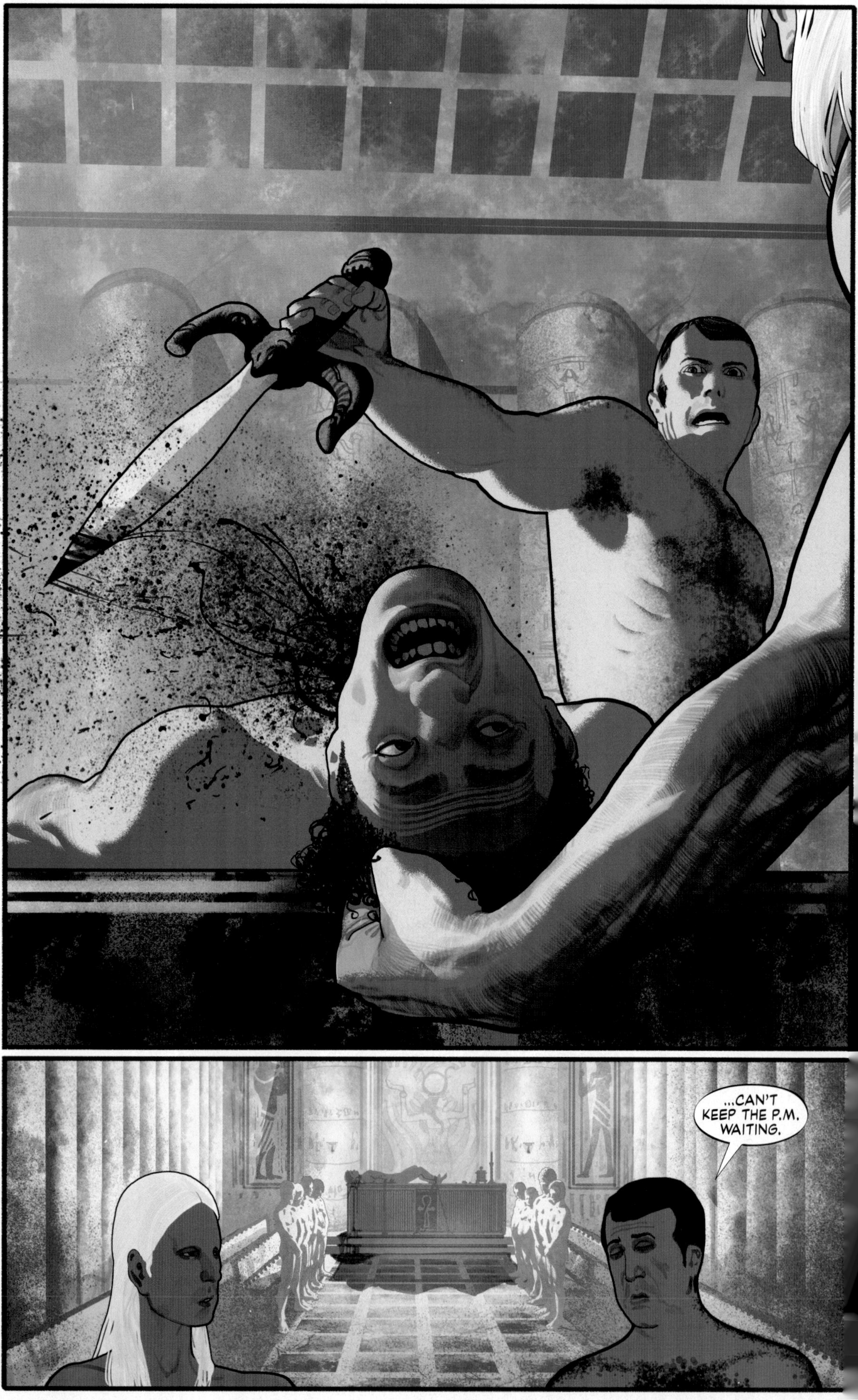

YOU DON'T HAVE TO DO THIS, YOU KNOW!
YES. YES, I'M AFRAID I DO.
BUT YOU'VE GONE ALL "HERO" NOW, HAVEN'T YOU?... HEARD YOU'D GONE TO THE GOOD, AND IF SO, WELL...YOUR KIND DOESN'T KILL.
HERO? WHY DOES EVERYONE THINK THAT I'D DO... BE...ANYTHING SO AVERAGE?
AND AS FOR KILLING, TRUTHFULLY THERE ARE TIMES I QUITE ENJOY IT.
NO, IN FACT, SCARLET TERROR--TERRIBLE NAME, BY THE WAY--YOU SIMPLY MUST DIE, THAT YOUR PASSING MAY SERVE A GREATER GOOD.
THOUGH I DOUBT THAT WILL BE MUCH CONSOLATION TO YOU.
GO'N N'DIE, W'DON'CHA? Y'MURDERER! PIECE O' DIRT, SO Y'ARE!
ELEGANTLY STATED, MY PAVEE FRIEND.
WAIT, NO! SILVERFIN! I KNOW YOU'RE A HERO, I READ THE PAPERS. MAGICAL GYPO.
OH, 'N I'LL CERTAINLY ENTERTAIN SPARIN' YOUR LIFE WI' THAT KIND O' TALK.
NO, NO--NO OFFENSE, I JUST MEANT THAT YOU'RE FOR THE SIDE OF GOOD.
'M F'WHAT I PERCEIVE AS GOOD-- THERE'S NO SET RULES, Y'IDGIT! 'N IT SEEMS T'ME A BLACKHEARTED WANKER LIKE YOU BEIN' DEAD N'ALL...
...'D BE A FINE THING.
IN THAT CASE, ARE YOU READY, FINBAR?
I'YM. DO THE HONORS.
PLEASE.

I'D SAY TALKING'S **DONE,** OLD FELLOW.
AYE, BEGONE W'YA!
SO, 'AT'S THE LAST O' THE FIVE, EH?
THANKFULLY. YOU'RE VERY **ARDENT,** BY THE BY--HAS ANYONE TOLD YOU THAT BEFORE?
MORE'N MOST. 'N THIS...BAD WORK TO BE SURE...IF'N THERE WEREN'T GOOD TO COME FROM IT, LIKE Y'SAY.
I HOPE YOU DON'T MIND ME ASKING, BUT... THAT BAG...YOUR MYSTERIOUS BAG... ARE YOU SURE...?

M'BAG O' FAVORS? 'TIS A THING O' WONDER. TEETH O' MY GRANDDA, HAIR OVVA WITCHFINDER TWO HUNDRED YEARS DEAD 'N GONE--DUG UP HIS GRAVE MESELF, SO I DID.
OH, AND A FEW OTHER THINGS FOR SEASONING--HEDGEHOG QUILLS DIPPED IN HEMLOCK 'N THE LIKE.
WHICH LEADS ME TO MY QUESTION... HAIR AND TEETH? IS THAT REALLY ENOUGH...I MEAN, ARE YOU SURE IT WILL WORK?
"WILL IT?" HE SAYS. WILL IT WORK? O' COURSE IT WILL, IT'S IRISH ROMANI MAGIC, AIN'T IT?
THEN... THANK YOU, FINBAR...SILVERFIN... AS EVER, YOU ARE MY STALWART FRIEND.

OH NO, DON' BE SO QUICK WITH THE BIG G'BYE. "STALWART"?... NO, US TRAVELERS DEAL IN **TRADE.** I HELPED YOU, SHADE...
...COMES A TIME, SOON OR FAR OFF AWAY, I'LL BE ASKIN' THE SAME.

WINGS+CHIPS
THAT'S FAIR, I SUPPOSE. YES, QUITE.
ANYWAYS, THIS PROBLEM O' YOURN... YOU'RE READY FOR'T...FOR WHAT'S AHEAD?
WELL, IT WOULD HELP IF I KNEW WHAT THE FUTURE HELD. I DON'T SUPPOSE...?
DIFFEREN' KIND O' MAGIC, MATE. I CAN MAKE SOME CALLS IF YOU'RE SERIOUS.

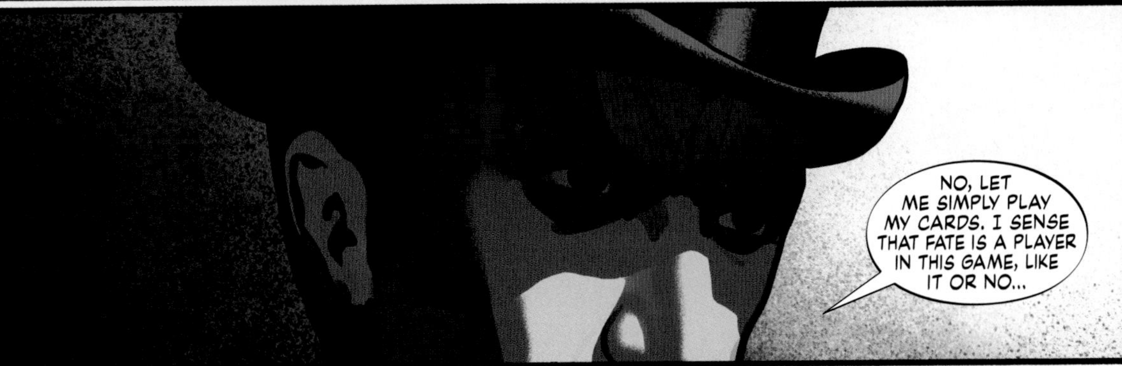
NO, LET ME SIMPLY PLAY MY CARDS. I SENSE THAT FATE IS A PLAYER IN THIS GAME, LIKE IT OR NO...

"...SO LET ME MEET HIM
WITH A FRESH FACE."
10

TRAVEL BOOKS
DOWN YOU GO, LORD CALDECOTT.

DUDLEY, MY BOY...IT'S TIME WE HAD A CHAT.
NO.
NOT YOU.

I'M NOT CROSS WITH YOU, BY THE WAY.
UNTIL I UNDERSTAND WHAT'S GOING ON, I'M WILLING TO CONCEDE THIS MAY **ALL** BE A SILLY MISUNDERSTANDING.

I'LL REFRAIN FROM THE OBVIOUS LECTURE ON HOW ONE SHOULD ADDRESS ONE'S ELDERS AND INSTEAD **IMPLORE** YOU TO PUT AN END TO THESE THEATRICS.
ARMED, BESPOKED HENCHMEN AT YOUR BECK AND CALL. MASONIC CABALS. I MEAN, IT'S HARDLY ORIGINAL...LIKE SOMETHING OUT OF A BULLDOG DRUMMOND ADVENTURE, OR ROHMER.
WHAT'S **NEXT,** FOR HEAVEN'S SAKE? THUGGEE ASSAS-SINS?

OH, NINJAS.
I SUPPOSE I SHOULD APPLAUD YOU KEEPING UP WITH THE TIMES IN THAT REGARD AT LEAST.

NOT THAT IT HELPS YOU.

TALK TO ME, DUDLEY. FOR THE LAST TIME, PLEASE. EXPLAIN YOURSELF.
MAY I BE ALLOWED TO SPEAK...
...MR. SWIFT?

AND YOU ARE...?

MILES ST. AUBREY. I'M A FELLOW MEMBER OF OUR CIRCLE.

WHAT, YOU AND DUDLEY? A CIRCLE? HOW QUAINT. YOU MAY SHARE THE SAME AREA OF LONDON, BUT YOU'RE HARDLY THE BLOOMSBURY GROUP.

A SURREPTITIOUS ROUTE... UTILIZING A FABLED, LOST AND MYSTERIOUS UNDERGROUND STATION... LEADING TO THIS SUBTERRANEAN LAIR.

I AM...THIS ***IS*** WHERE I THINK I AM, YES?

UNLESS YOUR GUESS IS WILDLY AWRY. I'D HAVE THOUGHT THE TUBE STATION ALONE WOULD GIVE IT AWAY. WHERE ELSE WOULD A GROUP LIKE OURS WITH LINKS TO ANCIENT EGYPTIAN LORE ABIDE...?

SO, DUDLEY, I GATHER YOU'VE BEEN USING THE CALDECOTT NAME AND EMPIRE FOR SOME SORT OF BLACKGUARDLY CONDUCT.

MUCH TO THE CONSTERNATION OF COUSIN DARNELL. DEAD NOW, AND GOOD RIDDANCE.
CHARMING.
BORING. DARNELL.

AND THESE ERRANT ACTIVITIES...I TAKE IT THIS PACK OF BORED OCCULTISTS ARE SOMEHOW EMBROILED IN YOUR MESS?
YOU MAKE US SOUND SO ORDINARY.
MASONS HAVE BEEN SHAKING HANDS AND DONNING APRONS FOR CENTURIES--I SHOULD KNOW. FOR THE MOST PART, IT'S A LOT OF SILLY DRESS-UP.

YES, AND IF WE WERE MASONS I'D AGREE WITH YOU.
YOU SEEM TO SHARE THE SAME TASTE IN DÉCOR.
THE MASON'S GRASP OF HISTORY IS A MIXED BAG AT BEST. WE FOUND THE TRUTH.

THE TRUTH? OH, I'M SURE. SO WHEN YOU'RE NOT BREAKING THE LAW, YOU'RE WORSHIPPING DEAD AND FORGOTTEN DEITIES. OH, THAT'S SO MUCH BETTER.

THAT'S THE THING, SWIFT...
...YOUR FIRST MISTAKE IS THINKING THOSE GODS ARE DEAD.
AND SECONDLY, WORSHIP THEM?

NOTHING OF THE KIND...
WAIT...

"...WE CONTROL THEM."
--MY POWERS-- GONE--

The Shade #10 variant cover art by Frazer Irving

IT WAS THEIR OWN *HUBRIS*...
"...IN THE END..."

"...THAT'S WHAT LED
TO THEIR DOWNFALL."

SHADOW PUPPETS

JAMES ROBINSON
WRITER

FRAZER IRVING
ARTIST & COLORIST

TODD KLEIN
LETTERER

TONY HARRIS
COVER ARTIST

THAT'S HOW GODS CAME TO KNOW THE FEEL OF SHACKLES.
I HAD SOUGHT OUT MY GREAT-GRANDSON DUDLEY, LORD CALDECOTT, WHO THROUGH A SERIES OF EVENTFUL DRAMAS I HAD COME TO LEARN WAS INVOLVED IN UNSAVORY CONDUCT..
TURNS OUT HE'S PART OF SOME SORT OF MASONIC CABAL...WHO SOMEHOW HAVE FANTASTIC EGYPTIAN BEINGS AT THEIR BECK AND CALL...WHO IN TURN SOMEHOW HAVE THE ABILITY TO DAMPEN MY SHADOWY TALENTS.
LONG/SHORT, I'M STUCK HERE REALIZING WHAT A SPINELESS MILKSOP MY OFFSPRING DUDLEY HAS BECOME WHILE BEING FORCED TO ENDURE THE SMUG DRONE OF HIS COLLEAGUE MILES ST. AUBREY.
EGADS, THE MAN LIKES TO TALK EVEN MORE THAN I DO.
GODS, YOU SAY? YOU'RE SURE? THEY LOOK PRETTY SOLVENT.
HONESTLY, I DON'T CARE WHAT THEY ARE. GODS. STAR TRAVELERS, PERHAPS... I'M SURE YOU'VE READ VON DÄNIKEN, OR AT LEAST KNOW HIS THEORIES.

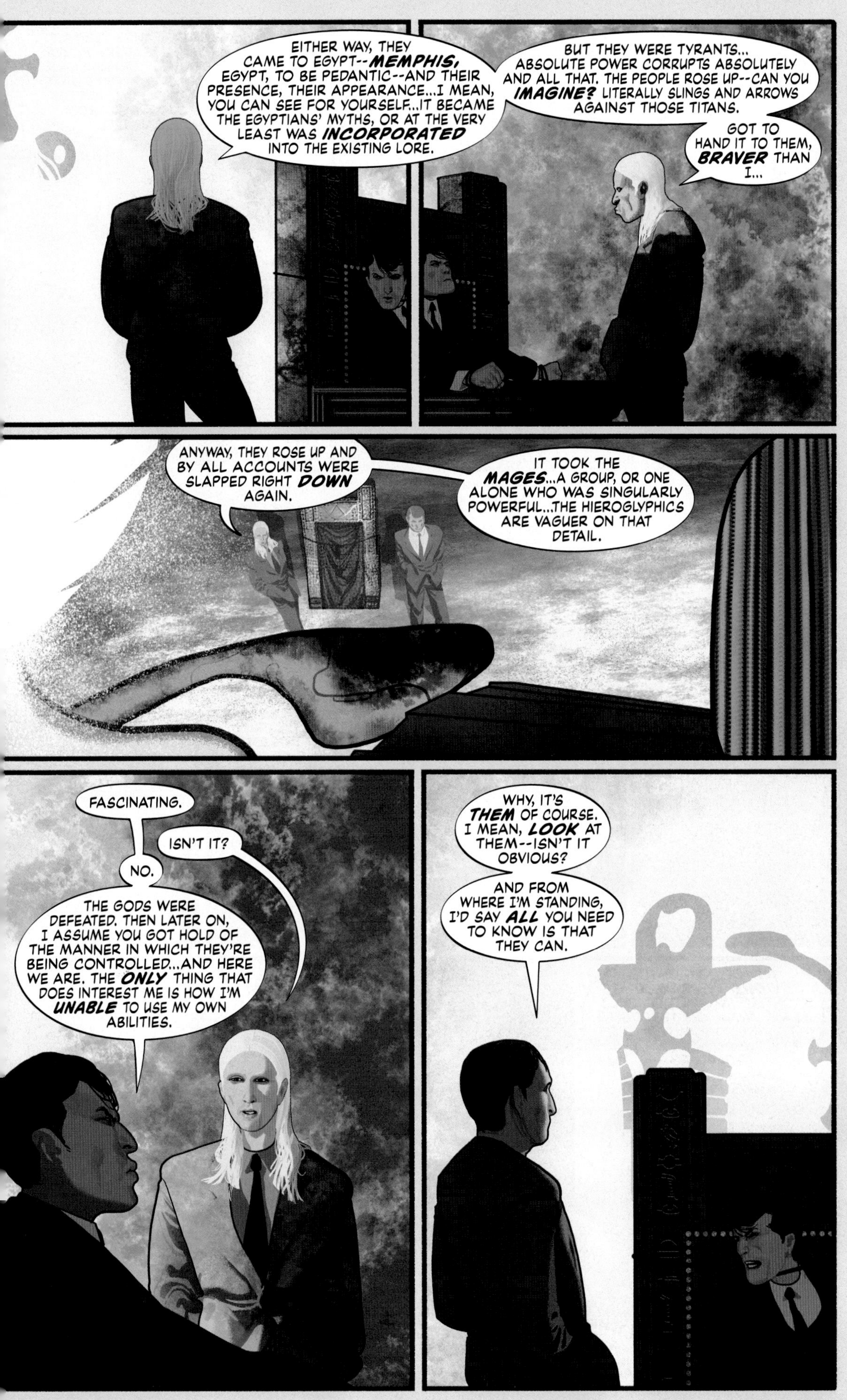
EITHER WAY, THEY CAME TO EGYPT--MEMPHIS, EGYPT, TO BE PEDANTIC--AND THEIR PRESENCE, THEIR APPEARANCE...I MEAN, YOU CAN SEE FOR YOURSELF...IT BECAME THE EGYPTIANS' MYTHS, OR AT THE VERY LEAST WAS INCORPORATED INTO THE EXISTING LORE.
BUT THEY WERE TYRANTS... ABSOLUTE POWER CORRUPTS ABSOLUTELY AND ALL THAT. THE PEOPLE ROSE UP--CAN YOU IMAGINE? LITERALLY SLINGS AND ARROWS AGAINST THOSE TITANS.
GOT TO HAND IT TO THEM, BRAVER THAN I...
ANYWAY, THEY ROSE UP AND BY ALL ACCOUNTS WERE SLAPPED RIGHT DOWN AGAIN.
IT TOOK THE MAGES...A GROUP, OR ONE ALONE WHO WAS SINGULARLY POWERFUL...THE HIEROGLYPHICS ARE VAGUER ON THAT DETAIL.
FASCINATING.
ISN'T IT?
NO.
THE GODS WERE DEFEATED. THEN LATER ON, I ASSUME YOU GOT HOLD OF THE MANNER IN WHICH THEY'RE BEING CONTROLLED...AND HERE WE ARE. THE ONLY THING THAT DOES INTEREST ME IS HOW I'M UNABLE TO USE MY OWN ABILITIES.
WHY, IT'S THEM OF COURSE. I MEAN, LOOK AT THEM--ISN'T IT OBVIOUS?
AND FROM WHERE I'M STANDING, I'D SAY ALL YOU NEED TO KNOW IS THAT THEY CAN.

AH, SO YOU'VE FOUND YOUR TONGUE, DUDLEY. I WAS BEGINNING TO THINK YOU'D SWALLOWED IT.
ME? NO, NOT AT ALL. IN FACT, LET'S EXCHANGE SOME ACCORD... OR LACK THEREOF BEFORE YOU'RE CONSIGNED TO WHATEVER FATE MILES DEEMS APPROPRIATE.

"WHATEVER FATE MILES DEEMS"? HOW MUCH THE LEADER--YOUR LEADER--IS HE? YOU'RE LORD CALDECOTT, FOR HEAVEN'S SAKE. HE'S...WHAT?...JUST SOME JUMPED-UP POMPOUS ASS, FROM WHAT I CAN TELL.

YOUR UNIQUE AND LENGTHY EXISTENCE HAS PROBABLY SHAPED AN EQUALLY UNIQUE YARDSTICK OF JUDGMENT FOR ALL MEN. BUT TO ME...TO MOST OF OUR GROUP, MILES ST. AUBREY IS A VERY CHARISMATIC AND PERSUASIVE FIGURE.
HE'S ALSO VERY EFFICIENT AT PROTECTING THE GROUP'S FINANCIAL INTERESTS AT HOME AND ABROAD.

GROUP? YOUR GROUP, DOES IT HAVE A NAME, AT LEAST?

NO. IT'S JUST "THE GROUP." WE VALUE ANONYMITY OVER THEATRICS.

YES, NOTHING THEATRIC--APART FROM RITES AND NINJAS AND SECRET ENTRYWAYS AND BIG EGYPTIAN GODS.

YOU HAVE A POINT.

AND OF COURSE, IT'S OBVIOUS THEY'RE WHAT ARE STUNTING MY ABILITIES. NO, I MEANT HOW ARE THEY DOING IT? I HAVE TO ADMIT I'M USED TO BEING INVINCIBLE IN THAT REGARD, SO--
YES, THE MIGHTY, MYSTERIOUS SHADE HELPLESS. MUST BE A SHOCK.
A SURPRISE. SHOCK? NO, THAT RARELY HAPPENS.

WELL, TO ANSWER YOU... I'M AFRAID I CAN'T.
TRUTHFULLY, THE ENTITIES ARE STILL A BIT OF A MYSTERY. I MEAN, WE TRIED TO PROBE THEM--FIGURATIVE "WE," 1936, BEFORE EITHER MYSELF OR DUDLEY WAS BORN--AND ALL WE SUCCEEDED IN DOING WAS KILLING ONE OF THE ENTITIES AND A LOT OF OUR BOFFINS.
YES...

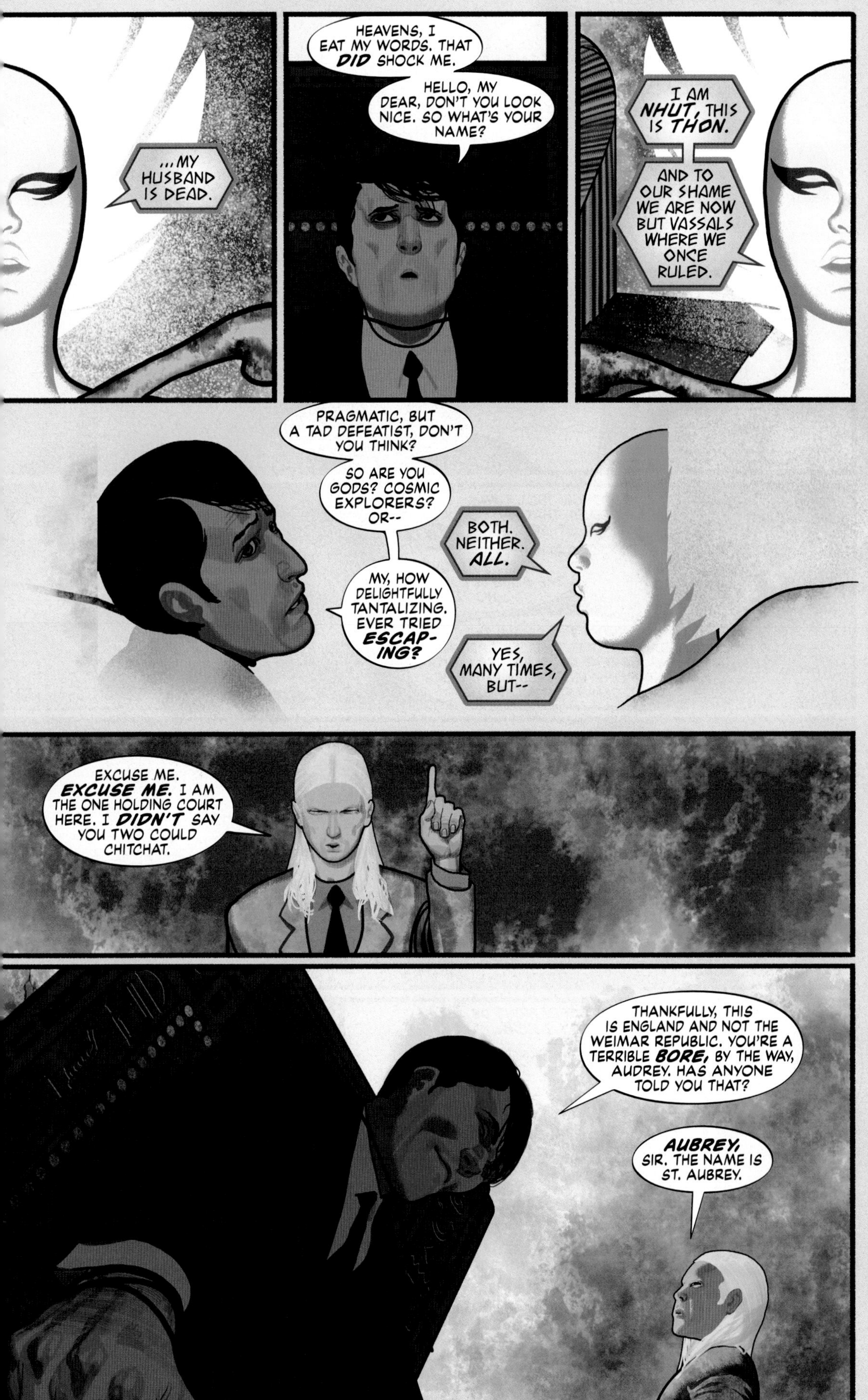
...MY HUSBAND IS DEAD.
HEAVENS, I EAT MY WORDS. THAT DID SHOCK ME.
HELLO, MY DEAR, DON'T YOU LOOK NICE. SO WHAT'S YOUR NAME?
I AM NHUT, THIS IS THON.
AND TO OUR SHAME WE ARE NOW BUT VASSALS WHERE WE ONCE RULED.
PRAGMATIC, BUT A TAD DEFEATIST, DON'T YOU THINK?
SO ARE YOU GODS? COSMIC EXPLORERS? OR--
BOTH. NEITHER. ALL.
MY, HOW DELIGHTFULLY TANTALIZING. EVER TRIED ESCAPING?
YES, MANY TIMES, BUT--
EXCUSE ME. EXCUSE ME. I AM THE ONE HOLDING COURT HERE. I DIDN'T SAY YOU TWO COULD CHITCHAT.
THANKFULLY, THIS IS ENGLAND AND NOT THE WEIMAR REPUBLIC. YOU'RE A TERRIBLE BORE, BY THE WAY, AUDREY. HAS ANYONE TOLD YOU THAT?
AUBREY, SIR. THE NAME IS ST. AUBREY.

THAT'S NOT EVEN THEIR FULL SIZE, BY THE WAY. THE GODS. THE DEVICE THAT CONTROLS THEM KEEPS THEM TO A MANAGEABLE SCALE. IT WAS FATHER WHO FOUND THEM, DID YOU KNOW THAT?
ALBERT.
YOU MET HIM, DIDN'T YOU?
YES, ONCE, 1901. I WAS REMINDED OF THAT FACT ONLY THE OTHER DAY.
WELL, HE DISCOVERED THE GODS IN EGYPT. 1920. NO, '21.
EGYPT WAS ALL THE RAGE AT THAT TIME, AS I RECALL, AND A GREAT MANY BRITISH GENTRY AND MONEYED TYPES WENT THERE LOOKING FOR ARTIFACTS.
TRUTH BE TOLD, I THINK DEAR OLD PATER WENT LOOKING FOR YOUNG BOYS IN THE KASBAH, BUT SOMEHOW IN THE COURSE OF HIS SORDID ESCAPADE HE GOT WORD OF AN UNOPENED PYRAMID.
HE NOTIFIED THE GROUP OF THAT ERA WHO SENT THEIR BULLY BOYS TO CLAIM IT. INSIDE WERE THE ENTITIES ALONG WITH THE DEVICE THAT SUBDUED THEM... SOMEHOW COMBINING ARCANE POWER WITH A CRUDE FORM OF CLOCKWORK NOT UNLIKE THE SORT OF THING FOUND IN ANCIENT PERSIA.
AND THESE GODS DO WHAT EXACTLY? KILL FOR YOU, RESHAPE THE WORLD, WHAT? I MEAN, THEY HAVE THE POWER TO SUBDUE ME, SO--
THEY BRING US LUCK.
I KNOW THAT SOUNDS DAFT, BUT ALL THEY DO...DON'T ASK ME HOW...IS EMIT AN ENERGY THAT AIDS OUR ENDEAVORS.
BUT IF THEY'RE JUST AIDING YOU IN BUSINESS, WHY THE ASSASSINS, THE SECRETS? I'M LOST.
AH, WELL, IT'S THE KIND OF BUSINESS. WE HAVE LEGITIMATE HOLDINGS, OBVIOUSLY, BUT THERE'S MONEY TO BE MADE IN THE ILLEGITIMATE, TOO.

DRUGS.
DRUGS. ARMS. CHILDREN. GERMS.
DUDLEY, IN GOD'S NAME!
OH, SHOCKED AGAIN? TWICE NOW? LET'S HAVE A GO AT A HAT TRICK, SHALL WE, DUDLEY? WHAT DO YOU SAY?
ARMS SALES ARE DOWN BECAUSE TERRORISM'S BEEN ON A SLIGHT DECLINE OF LATE. WE THOUGHT THAT SHOULD CHANGE. WE HAVE A DEAL WITH SOME ALGERIANS IN FRANCE--
THEY'RE DRUG DEALERS, SO THEY'RE CERTAINLY IN IT FOR THE HEROIN WE'RE SUPPLYING THEM, BUT THEY COULD BELIEVE IN A CAUSE, TOO--THESE THINGS CAN BE GRAY.
NOT THAT I CARE, NOT THAT ANYONE IN THE GROUP GIVES A DAMN. SUFFICE IT TO SAY, THE WORLD WILL BE REAWAKENED TO THE THREAT OF TERRORISM SOON.
SOON? WHEN SOON?
TODAY. THREE O'CLOCK TODAY. LES INVALIDES.
TOO LITTLE AND A TAD TOO LATE FOR YOU, I'D SAY.
YOU THINK SO? HMM. IF THERE'S BUT ONE REAL TRUTH I'VE LEARNED...
...IT'S THAT IT'S NEVER TOO LATE.

WAIT! HOLD ON...WHAT ARE YOU DOING? WHAT IS HE DOING?!
THON! HOW CAN HE DO THAT...FADING? STOP HIM!
HIS POWER. IT IS TOO GREAT.
AS THE MOMENTS PASS, IT SURPASSES OURS. WE NEED MORE OF OUR OWN ENERGY RETURNED TO US.
MORE. YES.
CARMICHAEL!
SIR.
CEDE THEIR POWER! JUST A LITTLE THOUGH, YOU HEAR ME?
SO THAT'S THE DEVICE DUDLEY MENTIONED, EH?
I'D HOPED THIS STUNT MIGHT AFFORD ME A GLIMPSE OF IT.

ALL TO KEEP ME FROM YOUR MASONIC GROUP...I ALWAYS THOUGHT THAT SORT OF NONSENSE ***ONLY*** EXISTED WITHIN THE PAGES OF CONSPIRACY THEORY PAPERBACKS PEOPLE BOUGHT FOR LONG TRAIN JOURNEYS.

AND AS FAR AS THE WHOLE "BROTHERHOOD" THING GOES, IT OCCURS TO ME I'VE ONLY MET THE TWO OF YOU.

VERY ***ELITE.*** YOUR INITIATIONS MUST BE EXCRUCIATING.

"...IT'S ***CEREMONY.***"

SEE. LOTS OF US.

NOT YOU, WE KNOW THAT'S IMPOSSIBLE-- AND BESIDES, IT WOULD DEFEAT THE PURPOSE OF GETTING YOU IN THE FIRST PLACE.
MILES, LOOK AT HIM...

...WHAT'S HAPPENING?

CARMICHAEL, I'LL CUT OUT YOUR EYES MYSELF IF YOU LET THIS HAPPEN AGAIN. MORE POWER!...

...THE GODS!... GIVE THEM WHAT THEY NEED OR WE'LL LOSE THIS SNEAKY BASTARD!

LOSE ME? WITH ALL THE MALE NUDITY IN EVIDENCE, I'M SCARED TO ASK WHAT YOU'LL DO IF YOU KEEP ME.

DON'T FLATTER YOURSELF. YOU'LL BE TESTED, OF COURSE. YOUR IMMORTALITY... OBVIOUSLY YOU SEE HOW THAT COULD BE DESIRABLE TO US IF IT CAN BE REPLICATED.

AND THEN THERE'S YOUR SHADOW POWER. WE'LL HAVE SCIENTISTS ON ALL OF IT BY TEATIME.

BUT FIRST WE BAPTIZE THE NEW ENDEAVOR. OUR ACQUISITION--YOU--WITH THE BLOOD OF AN INNOCENT.
ALTHOUGH THIS ONE'S BEEN ON THE STREET FOR A WHILE, SO "INNOCENT" IS PROBABLY A RELATIVE TERM.
IT'S ONLY SYMBOLIC, AFTER ALL.
DUDLEY, **PLEASE** DON'T TAKE HER LIFE.
I'M NOT WITHOUT MY MURDEROUS SIDE, BUT EVEN I LIKE TO THINK THAT NO DEATH I'VE CAUSED HAS BEEN NEEDLESS.
GREAT-GRANDFATHER, I'M SORRY HOW THINGS ARE.
BUT THEY ARE.
MILES!...

...HE'S STARTING TO FADE!
AGAIN?

MORE POWER! GIVE THE GODS MORE POWER!

SIGH

SUDDENLY I'VE A FEELING YOU'LL MOMENTARILY HAVE MORE THAN ME TO CONCERN YOU.
WHAT DO YOU MEAN?

WELL, I'M NOT ONE TO TELL YOU YOUR BUSINESS, GENTLEMEN...

...BUT IS GIVING THE GODS BACK THAT WHICH WAS TAKEN THE SMARTEST MOVE?

CARMICHAEL! WHAT ARE YOU WAITING--?

"...WHAT HAVE YOU DONE?"

HARRIS

The Shade #11 variant cover art by Frazer Irving

QUITE A SPECTACLE, I CAN TELL YOU.
EGYPTIAN GODS? ALIENS? (NO IDEA, REALLY)...
...LAYING WASTE TO LONDON...

...AND FIGHTING ITS HEROES.

IT OCCURS TO ME THAT THE MAN I WAS AT ONE TIME WOULD HAVE FELT SCORN FOR THESE MYSTERY MEN...

...I WOULD HAVE LAUGHED AT THEIR MEAGER TRIUMPHS AND VALIANT FAILURES.
THE MAN I WAS WOULD HAVE--
I'D HAVE--

INSTEAD I'M NOT SURE EXACTLY WHAT I FEEL.
HMM. WHAT ELSE?

GOOD LUCK, BEAUMONT, SIR.
NO "SIR," JUST "BEAUMONT." BUT THANK YOU...ABOUT LUCK, I MEAN. I'VE A FEELING I'LL NEED IT.
...OH YES, I SEE AN INDESTRUCTIBLE MAN...

...LEAP FROM THE SKY AND FALL...
...DOWN...
...DOWN...

...TO NO AVAIL.
AND WITH THAT--WITH BEAUMONT, THE HEROES' LAST HOPE, SWATTED ASIDE (FROM WHAT I COULD TELL ROUGHLY IN THE DIRECTION OF DAGENHAM)...

THE BAD LIBRARIANS

JAMES ROBINSON
WRITER

FRAZER IRVING
ARTIST & COLORIST

TODD KLEIN
LETTERER

TONY HARRIS
COVER ARTIST

I SUPPOSE I'VE BEEN FORTUNATE EXPERIENCING ALL THAT I HAVE OF LATE.
FROM MY ADVENTURE IN AUSTRALIA, I'D LEARNED TO OPEN THE DOOR TO DREAMTIME.
IN SPAIN I'D DISCOVERED A HITHERTO UNKNOWN LEVEL TO MY OWN SHADOWY POWERS...
...AND I'D BEEN REMINDED OF THE POWER OF THE PENTAGRAM.
FORTUNATELY, I'D HAD ENOUGH MISADVENTURES IN LONDON IN MY INITIAL TRAVAILS, KILLED ENOUGH PEOPLE IN ENOUGH LOCATIONS...THAT I'D BEEN ABLE TO CREATE A FIVE-POINTED STAR TO SURROUND THE CITY FROM AMONG THE SITES OF MY MANY PAST WRONGDOINGS (MUCH LIKE THE INQUISITOR HAD ATTEMPTED IN BARCELONA).

ALL IT THEN REQUIRED WAS REANOINTING THEM WITH FRESH BLOOD (OF VILLAINS AND NE'ER-DO-WELLS BETTER OFF DEAD, I ASSURE YOU).
NEEDING A DEITY TO HONOR IN THIS RITE, AND NOT BEING A CHRISTIAN, THIS BAPTISM WAS BLESSED WITH A SPELL EVOKING SCATHACH, A PAGAN GOD THAT I BECAME AWARE OF AT THE TIME OF MY ORIGIN.
SAID SPELL PERFORMED BY SILVERFIN, IRISH ROMANI MAGE AND ALL-AROUND HANDY FELLOW.
HOW DID I KNOW I'D NEED THE PENTAGRAM IN THE FIRST PLACE?
I DIDN'T.

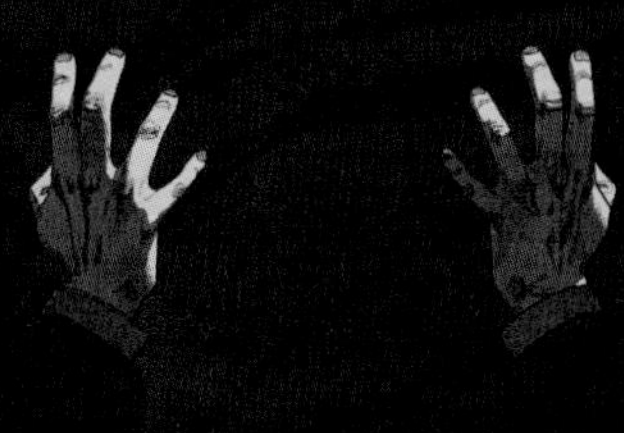

BUT IF I'VE LEARNED ANYTHING IN MY TIME...IN ALL MY TIME LIVED..
...IT'S THAT IT'S ALWAYS BETTER TO HAVE A PLAN B THAN NOT. YES, I KNEW I'D BE FIGHTING SOME KIND OF EVIL, AND THE PENTAGRAM THUS ENLIVENED WOULD GIVE ME AN EDGE.
SUCH BEING THE CASE IN COMBAT WITH THESE MONOLITHS.
UNFORTUNATELY FOR ME NOW...

...I HAVE TO DO THE ACTUAL COMBAT PART.
Tsk.
I HATE THIS SORT OF NONSENSE.

HAVE TO BE SHARPISH TOO, CAN'T DALLY...
...THEIR POWER IS TOO **STRONG** FOR ME TO CONTAIN THEM MUCH LONGER.
THEIR FREEDOM HAS MADE THEM--WHAT'S THE WORD? UNBRIDLED? NO, **UN-FOCUSED.** THEY'RE NOT THINKING TO SUPPRESS MY POWER...
...THEY **CAN'T** BE, OR I WOULDN'T BE ABLE TO DO WHAT I AM.

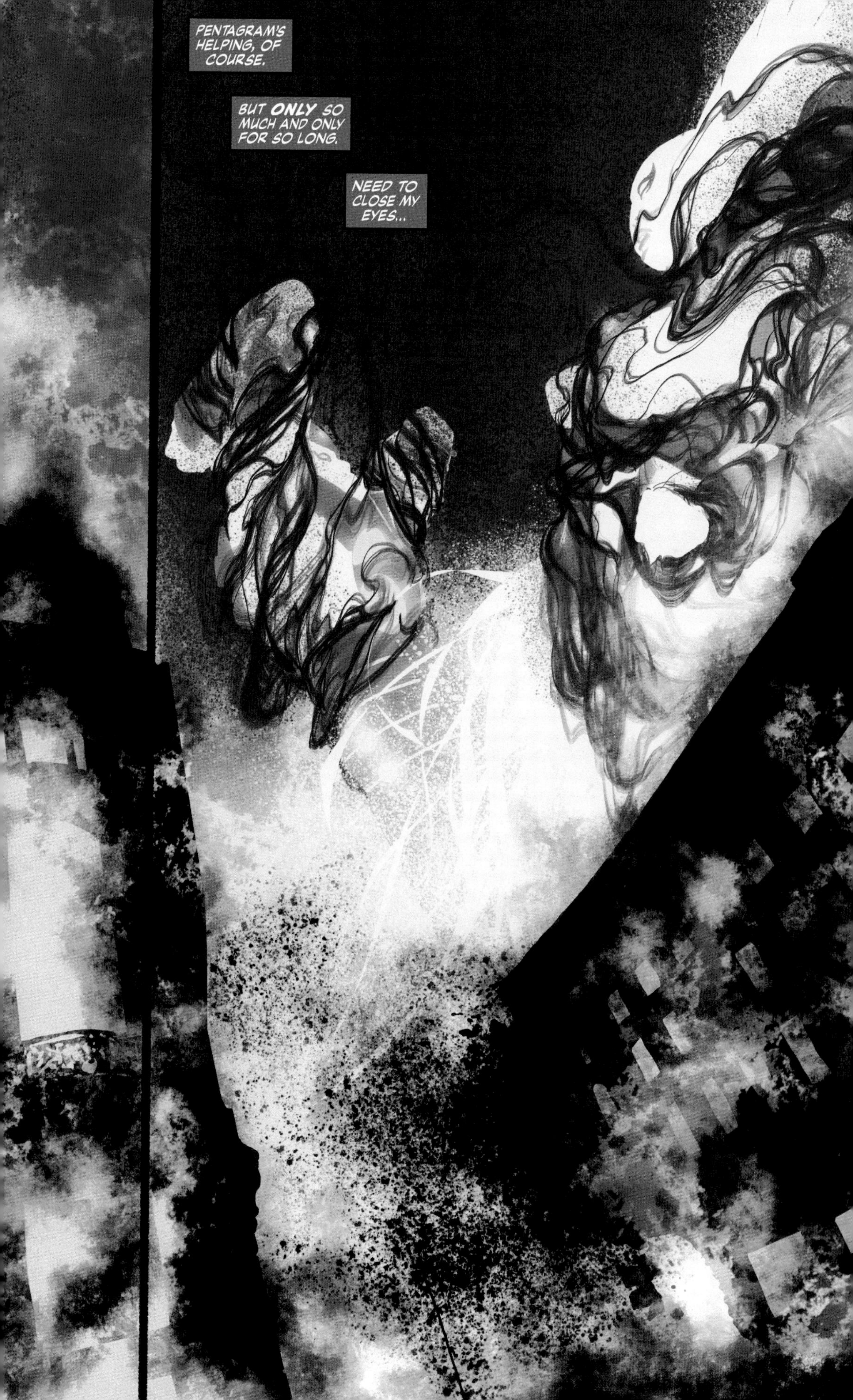
PENTAGRAM'S HELPING, OF COURSE.
BUT ONLY SO MUCH AND ONLY FOR SO LONG.
NEED TO CLOSE MY EYES...

...AND CONCENTRATE.
YES! IT'S WORKING!

I WAS PRETTY SURE I **COULDN'T** DEFEAT THEM OUTRIGHT, BUT I **CAN** AT LEAST **TRANSPORT** THEM AWAY.

INTO DREAMLAND.. THE DREAMING... ANOTHER PLANE...

...ANOTHER PLACE.

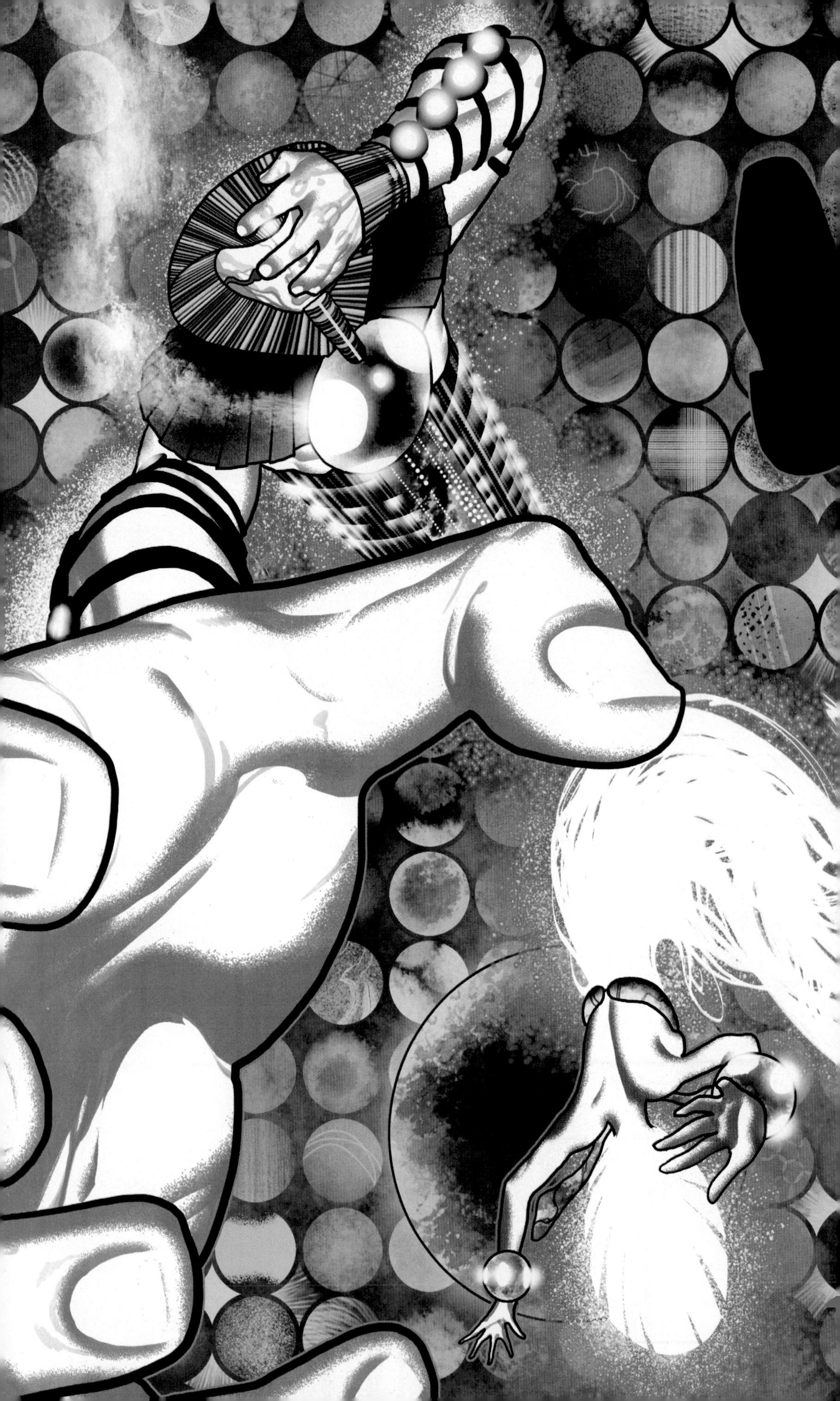

...HAVE TO SAY THIS ISN'T QUITE WHAT I IMAGINED.

WHERE ARE WE?
WHAT IS THIS PLACE?
WHAT HAVE YOU DONE?
YES, WISH I HAD THE ANSWER TO THAT ONE MYSELF, BUT I DON'T, I'M AFRAID. NO CLUE.
IT ISN'T THE DREAMING, I CAN SENSE THAT MUCH. NOR THE DARKNESS, OBVIOUSLY. I THINK YOUR PRESENCE, YOUR POWER HAS SENT US TO SOME KIND OF POCKET DIMENSION OR VOID, BUT I'M LOATH TO GUESS WHERE. HAVE TO SAY, THOUGH--
HOLD ON, THIS IS ABSURD! WHY AM I BEING SO CIVIL WITH THE PAIR OF YOU? YOU'VE DESTROYED LONDON, THE CITY OF MY PAST. LONDON! NOT TO MENTION THE COUNTLESS INNO-CENT LIVES YOU'VE TAKEN!
YOU HAVE QUESTIONS? I'M THE ONE WITH QUESTIONS! WHAT ARE YOU EXACTLY? I KNOW YOU'RE MONSTERS... MANIACS...BUT...
...ARE YOU EVEN FROM EARTH? ARE YOU FROM THE STARS, FROM OUTER SPACE? COME ON, OUT WITH IT!
ANOTHER PLACE? NO. YES. OUR WORLD IS BEYOND TIME, BEYOND SPACE.
WE WERE SENT TO YOUR WORLD... TO "EARTH" TO VIEW AND REPORT.
THAT WAS OUR MISSION, TASK, LIFE-TASK-- UPON THE DISCOVERY OF A NEW WORLD.

IN ORDER TO CONQUER?
NO, TO CHRONICLE. WE ARE FROM THE HIDDEN LIBRARY. WE SEE TRUTHS AND NOTHING MORE.
"HIDDEN LIBRARY"?
OF THE CRIMSON CORRIDOR.
IN THE SAD HOUSE.
PRESUME. ASSUME.
PLEASE TELL ME THAT'S A METAPHOR OR AN IMBALANCE OF TRANSLATION. OTHER-WISE--
I'M IMMORTAL... AS OF HALFWAY THROUGH THE 19TH CENTURY AT LEAST... AND COMPARED TO THOSE WHO LIVE AND DIE, I SOMETIMES MUSE AND MARVEL AT ALL I'VE SEEN...THE SHEER BREADTH OF MY EXPERIENCES.
YOU'RE OLDER BY CENTURIES, I CAN'T IMAGINE WHAT YOU'VE WITNESSED.
YOU CAN'T IMAGINE. YES. NO. NOTHING COMPARES.
WE HAVE SEEN CULTURES... PEOPLE AND BEINGS... AMAZING WORLDS...WE HAVE SEEN THEM LIVE AND GROW AND DIE FORGOTTEN.
WE HAVE SEEN STARS BORN FROM DARKNESS THAT IN YOUR NIGHT SKY GLOWED WHITE/BRIGHT ONCE AND ARE NOW NO MORE.
ALL THE BEAUTY AND ALL THE UGLY REALITY BEHIND THAT BEAUTY.
ALL RIGHT, YOU CAME, YOU CHRONICLED. FINE. NOT SO FINE: YOU DECIDING IT WAS MORE FUN TO LAY WASTE TO CITIES. WHY THE CHANGE?

OUR MEANS OF ARRIVAL TO YOUR PLANET... OUR PORTAL WAS DAMAGED. THERE WAS NO WAY BACK FOR US. EGYPT THEN, HOT AND BRIGHT. MORE IMPORTANT, IT WAS...UNLIKE. THIS FACT ANGERED US AND MADE US CRUEL. OUR CRUELTY LED TO A REVOLT BY YOUR KIND AND WE WERE SNARED.
TRAPPED.
THE CARNAGE YOU WITNESSED WAS OUR REVENGE ON THE RACE OF MEN WHO HELD OUR CHAINS.
WELL, ANCIENT EGYPT ISN'T MODERN LONDON, BUT THAT APPARENTLY DOESN'T MATTER TO YOU. NOR DO THE COUNTLESS THOUSANDS OF INNOCENTS YOU'VE MURDERED.
GODS? NEW GODS, GREAT GODS? WHY, YOU'RE NOTHING BUT SHAMBLING CHILDREN IN FANCY DRESS!
SIGH
AT LEAST I HAVE YOU HERE AWAY FROM LONDON AND ITS PEOPLE.
AND SO YOU SEEK TO BRING JUSTICE UPON US BY CONSIGNING US TO THIS UNENDING EXISTENCE... THIS LIMBO? IS THAT YOUR INTENTION? JUSTICE IS BUT A FRAYED HEM IN THE TAPESTRY OF EVERYTHING.
ALL RIGHT, LET'S SAY THERE WAS A WAY TO SEND YOU HOME. HOW DO YOU KNOW "HOME" HASN'T BECOME A...A...HOW DID YOU PHRASE IT? A STAR GONE DARK, OR WHATEVER YOU SAID?
PERHAPS. IF SO, THEN...I DO NOT KNOW... IF SO--
YOU DO KNOW, NHUT. YOU KNOW AS DO I THAT IF IT LIVES STILL, THEN WE DIE.
WAIT, HOLD ON. WHAT DID YOU JUST SAY?
TO CATALOGUE... THIS WAS OUR INSTRUCTION, BUT INSTEAD WE HAVE BROKEN THAT TENET. OUR IMAGES AND WAYS, OUR LORE, SOME OF IT IS NOW A PART OF YOUR HISTORY. OUR LEGEND LIVES ON ALONGSIDE THE OLD DEITIES OF THEN, BOTH REAL AND IMAGINED.
FOR THAT TRANSGRESSION OUR LIVES ARE DUST IF WE RETURN--THIS I KNOW.
BUT YOU STILL WANT TO GO BACK?
OF COURSE--HOME IS HOME. BETTER TO DIE THERE THAN LIVE AMONG YOUR RACE, SO STRANGE AND SMALL AND ARTLESS.
I THOUGHT MYSELF AMORAL-- NO, "THOUGHT"? I AM. I AM THE SHADE... I...
...I AM...THE... SHADE...
...AND YET...
...TO LIVE A LIFE EVERLASTING IS TO VALUE THOSE OF A SHORTER SPAN OF YEARS, I'VE COME TO SEE THAT. OF LATE.
BUT I SENSE NOT A JOT OF REMORSE FOR YOUR ACTIONS IN EITHER OF YOU.
AND BY GOD, I WANT YOU GONE FROM ME.

I'M NOT THE EXPERT IN ANY WAY ON WHERE WE ARE. I'M NOT AN ABORIGINE. I DON'T EVEN KNOW IF BEING ABORIGINE MATTERS IN THIS INSTANCE.
BUT I CAN FEEL IT SUDDENLY...I CAN SENSE IT, CAN'T YOU?... THAT IF WE TRY TOGETHER...IF WE CONCENTRATE AND TRY, WE CAN GET YOU ON THE PATHWAY HOME. AND MAY YOUR OWN WORLD LOVE YOU OR KILL YOU, I AM NOTHING OF A MIND.
STILL, NOW...
...BE STILL.

AND THAT WAS THAT?
YES, CAN YOU BELIEVE IT?
THEY LEFT WITHOUT A THANK YOU OR A NOD OR A TIP OF THE HAT. DISGRACEFUL.
AYE, WHO'DA GUESSED INTER-DIMENSIONAL CREATURES'D BE SO RUDE.
I DON'T KNOW IF YOU'RE BEING SERIOUS OR SARCASTIC.
N'COMIN' FROM YOU, THAT'S RICH.
SO, Y'OFF?
I ADMIT I MISS OPAL AND ALL IT HOLDS, BUT NO. I'LL TARRY HERE A WHILE LONGER.
ONE MORE THING TO DO.

I WAS **SAD** TO KILL DUDLEY.

DID HE DESERVE IT? YES, **ABSOLUTELY,** BUT HE WAS STILL MY BLOOD.

IT SET ME TO WONDERING, THIS, HIS DEATH...IF WHETHER THINGS MIGHT HAVE BEEN DIFFERENT HAD I NOT BECOME THE SHADE.

IF I'D LIVED AND DIED IN VICTORIAN LONDON... WOULD MY CHILDREN AND THEIRS HAVE WALKED A GENTLER AND LESS EVENTFUL ROAD?

BUT IT'S THE FOOL WHO PONDERS ON "WHAT IFS" AND "MIGHT HAVE BEENS" FOR OVERLY LONG.

I DID BECOME...I **AM** THE SHADE. THE EVENTS THAT CREATED ME HAPPENED. AND YOU KNOW...

...PERHAPS IT IS TIME I PUT QUILL TO PAPER AND RELATED THOSE GHASTLY EVENTS SO THAT, AIRED OUT, THEY MIGHT FINALLY REST.

The Shade #12 variant cover art by Gene Ha & Art Lyon

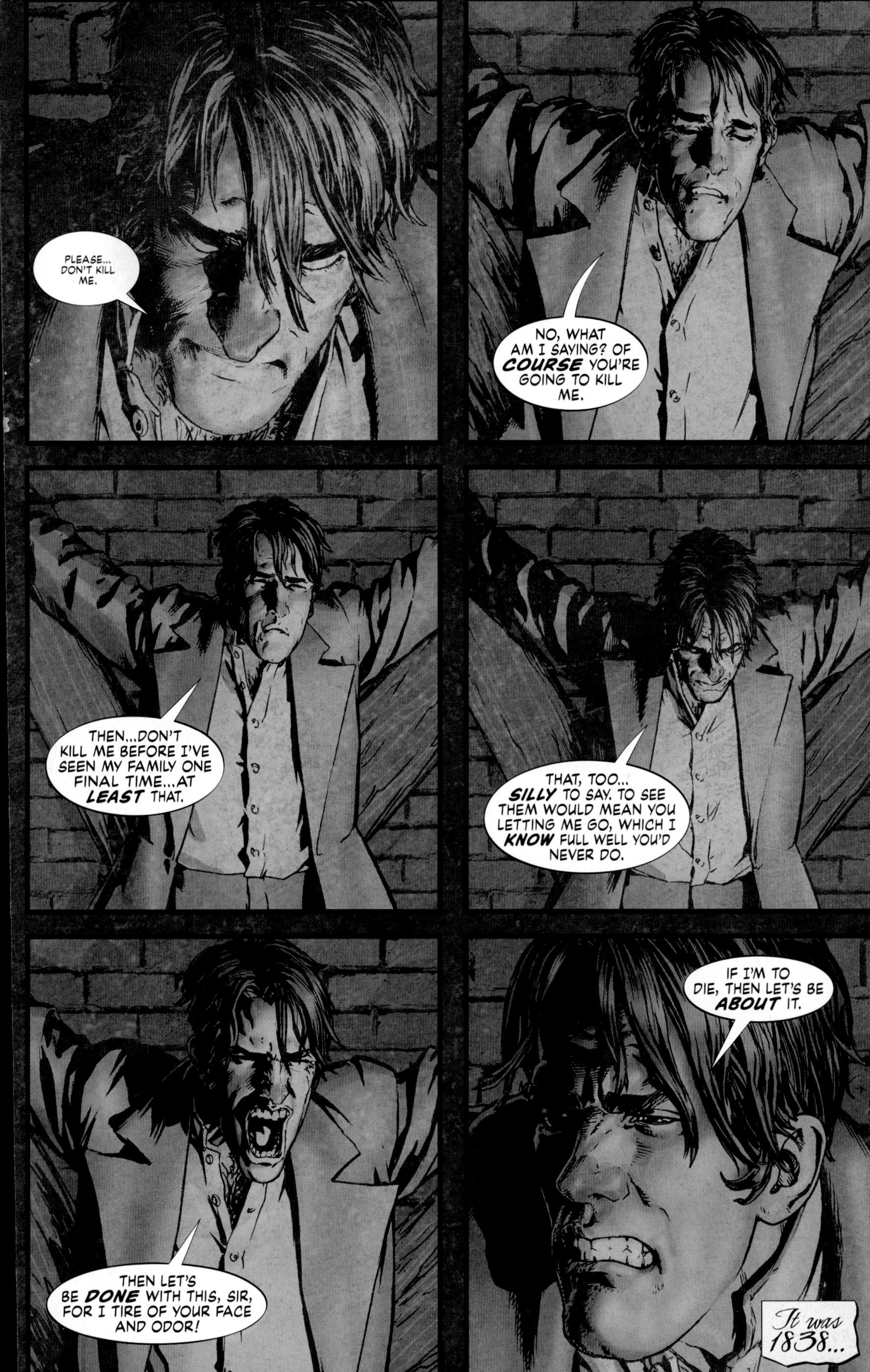
PLEASE...
DON'T KILL
ME.
NO, WHAT
AM I SAYING? OF
COURSE YOU'RE
GOING TO KILL
ME.
THEN...DON'T
KILL ME BEFORE I'VE
SEEN MY FAMILY ONE
FINAL TIME...AT
LEAST THAT.
THAT, TOO...
SILLY TO SAY. TO SEE
THEM WOULD MEAN YOU
LETTING ME GO, WHICH I
KNOW FULL WELL YOU'D
NEVER DO.
THEN LET'S
BE DONE WITH THIS, SIR,
FOR I TIRE OF YOUR FACE
AND ODOR!
IF I'M TO
DIE, THEN LET'S BE
ABOUT IT.
It was
1838...

TIMES PAST: 1838
Family Ties Part I
James Robinson writer
Gene Ha artist
Art Lyon colorist
Todd Klein letterer
Tony Harris cover artist
...and London Town was a jewel that I, Richard Swift, enjoyed holding up to the light.
And yes, I know the city wasn't that way for everyone. To the poor, I'm sure it seemed more Hell than haven.
But my business had for some years now assured me a steady income.
And more importantly—no... most importantly, the thing that for me made London shine...
...was my family.

I will always, if I live but another day or another century...

...recall the aroma of my wife Enid's cooking.

We had a servant, Dopsy—clean and tidy, if a tad slow... and yet my dear wife refused to let her or anyone at the oven but herself.

And coming home to Enid's delicious creations made even the darkest, dreariest night seem brighter.

That and her smile and her kisses.

HOW MANY SHILLINGS IN A GUINEA, SAM?

UM. I...I NEED TO COUNT. I THINK I KNOW... UM...

COME, COME, LAD, YOU NEED TO ***KNOW,*** NOT "THINK YOU DO," IN THE WORLD OF FINANCE.

TWENTY-ONE, FATHER! TWENTY-ONE SHILLINGS!!
THAT'S RIGHT, SON. MY, AND WHAT A CLEVER BOY YOU ARE.
My boys? Ah, well there...
I confess to a vague guilt, in that I favored Sam so much over John, the newborn.
Sam, the elder, was my favorite at that time. He was becoming his own little person, you see.
We'd talk and take long strolls through the park... sometimes sail the model boat I'd gotten him the Christmas before last. He was my son and my friend both.
John was a mewling thing, still hungry for his mother's nipple, and who in hindsight I'm ashamed to admit I didn't pay much mind to. That might have changed... probably would have, of course...
...had I been there to see him grow.
But we were a happy family. Indeed, I was certainly most content. And as Richard Swift, my wife's love meant everything to me.
NOW QUICKLY TAKE YOUR SEAT. YOUR MOTHER'S WORKED HARD ON THIS ROAST, AND I'D HATE TO SEE IT GO COLD BEFORE IT'S EATEN.

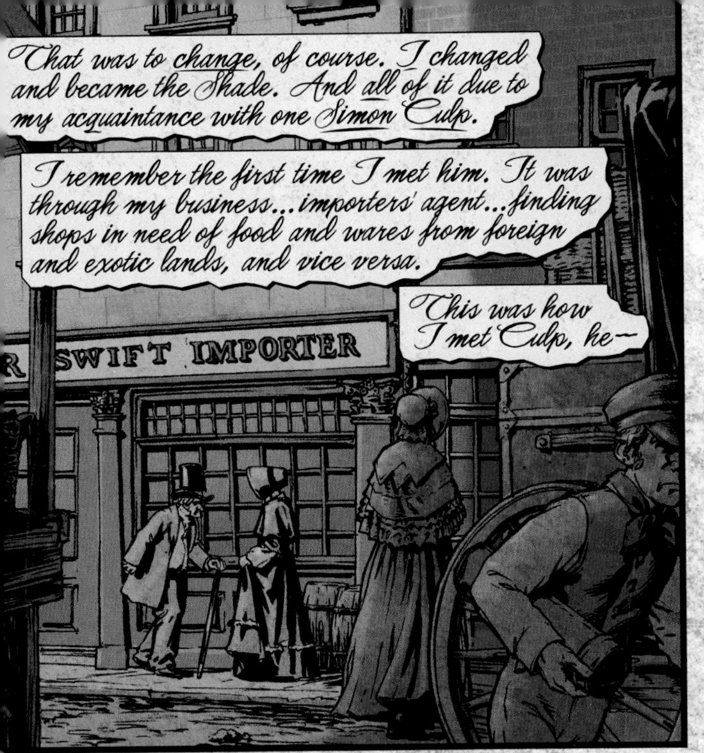
That was to change, of course. I changed and became the Shade. And all of it due to my acquaintance with one Simon Culp.
I remember the first time I met him. It was through my business... importers' agent... finding shops in need of food and wares from foreign and exotic lands, and vice versa.
This was how I met Culp, he—
SWIFT IMPORTER

No, I'm skipping ahead. One other player in the drama I should accord mention of first—my friend, the writer Charles Dickens.

I met Charles in a coffee house, no mystery there. I liked his spark, he liked my wit, and so a friendship grew.
He'd chance by my office from time to time to chat of the day's events or sometimes to relate his ideas for a story if some aspect of it wasn't completely to his liking.

YES, YES, I KNOW YOU LIKE PICKWICK. YOU'VE TOLD ME. EVERYONE'S TOLD ME HOW MUCH THEY LIKE PICKWICK. SCROOGE AND OLIVER, TOO. BUT IT'S ALL SO LIGHT IN COMPARISON TO MY LITERARY DESIGNS.
THEN WHAT STORY HAVE YOU IN MIND TO TELL?
I HAVE THE BEGINNINGS OF ONE IDEA, DICK...SET IN THE PAST DURING THE GORDON RIOTS AND A MUCH DARKER TALE.
And so Charles was there that day...

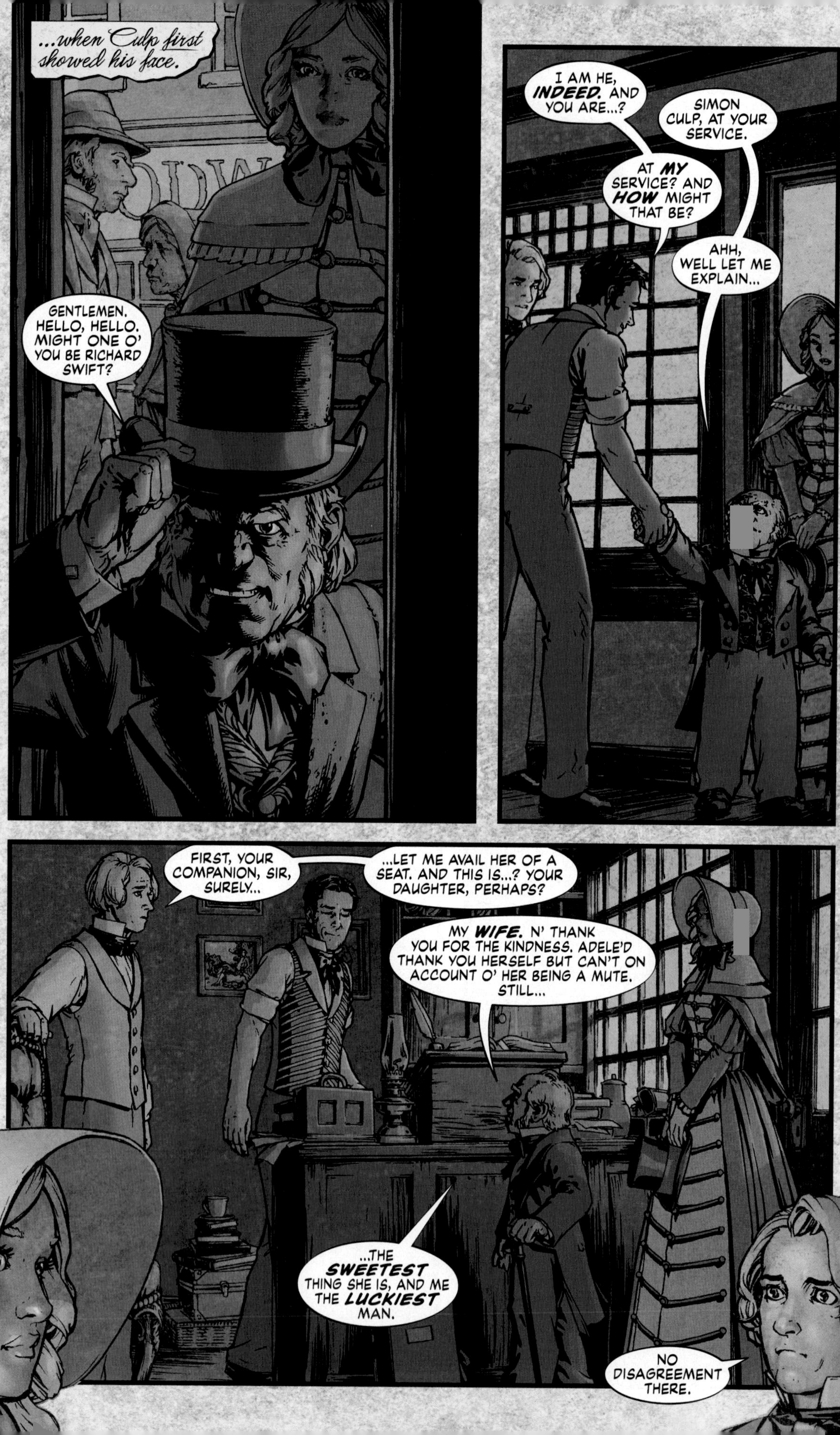

FIRST, YOUR COMPANION, SIR, SURELY...

...LET ME AVAIL HER OF A SEAT. AND THIS IS...? YOUR DAUGHTER, PERHAPS?

MY WIFE. N' THANK YOU FOR THE KINDNESS. ADELE'D THANK YOU HERSELF BUT CAN'T ON ACCOUNT O' HER BEING A MUTE. STILL...

...THE SWEETEST THING SHE IS, AND ME THE LUCKIEST MAN.

NO DISAGREEMENT THERE.

NOW, PLEASANTRIES ASIDE, GENTS...

...THERE'S TALK AMONG THE FOLK OF THE DOCKS AND ALONG THAMES WATER THAT SAYS YOU'RE A MAN WITH A RARE AND RESOURCEFUL TALENT, MR. SWIFT.

I'M NOT ONE TO DISAGREE, MR. CULP, BUT I MUST AT LEAST ASK TO WHICH TALENT IT IS YOU REFER.

WHY, THE PROCURING OF EXOTIC ITEMS. FRUITS AND TEA, SPICES, FURS AND SUCH.

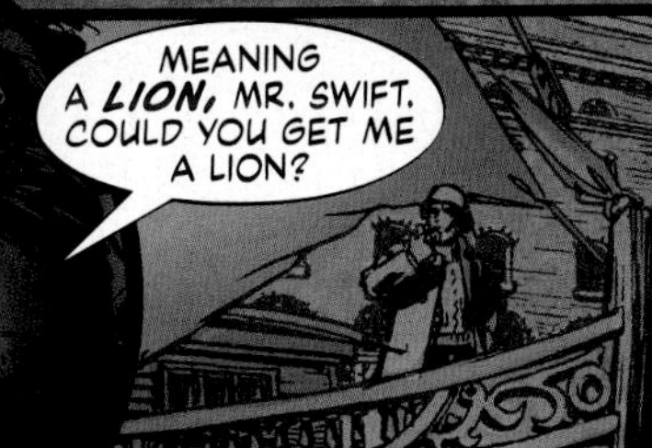

I accepted the undertaking despite Culp offering me no explanation as to why he wanted the animal.

I suppose it was the challenge of acquiring the cat, not to mention the not-inconsiderable coin he offered for my efforts.

I would see Culp periodically after that as he inquired on my progress and at other times merely to inquire upon my well-being.

I found him fascinating. Midgets and dwarfs were no strangers to London streets at that time, so my enchantment stemmed from another more magnetic aspect of the man.

His manner—no, no—his essence.

As if he hungered for something that even he himself could neither define nor imagine.

Charles did not approve.

IT'S NOT HIS SIZE, IT'S HIS MANNER, FOR HEAVEN'S SAKE. CAN'T YOU SEE?

AND HIS WIFE...**BARELY** A CHILD, AND MUTE? I FEAR THE GIRL IS SIMPLE AND IN THAT BRUTE'S CLUTCHES.

THE MAN'S NO GOOD!

He'd later depict Dick Swiveller, the character he based upon me in "The Old Curiosity Shop," as someone who was easily led, so I suppose Charles saw me for the fellow I was at that time.

The added lure of Culp for me...a traveler he, this little man...East as far as Markovia, South as far as blue Mediterranean waters.
TOWERS THAT STRETCH UP TO HEAVEN--SEEMED LIKE, AT LEAST--'COURSE, WITH MY HEIGHT A LOT DOES--HAHA! BIG OLD GUARDS THEY HAD, TOO. MEAN COVES, ALL BRASS ARMOR AND HARD STARES.
True, he hadn't ventured to the Dark Continent, but he'd at least seen lions and elephants among the pets of a moneyed bey in Constantinople.
And so the days...and indeed weeks passed as Culp and I...

SO, "BARNABY RUDGE"--QUAINT TITLE, I'LL GIVE YOU THAT.
QUAINT? I'D HOPED FOR MORE THAN QUAINT, DICK. HEAVENS!
...and Charles and I...

Culp was delighted.
NO, DICKIE, LUV, YOU MUST, YOU ABSOLUTELY MUST COME. IT'S A RIGHT OLD SPREAD. IT'S A GALA.
RUM SPOT TO HAVE IT, I'LL GIVE YOU THAT. STILL... MY CLIENT--WEALTHY, POWERFUL CLIENT--HE INSISTS.
What did I expect? I'm not sure. Shaking the hand of a wealthy man I'd helped... how could that be bad?

Have I told you I wasn't the man I am today? Dickens knew, of course...
LEAVE YOU? OF COURSE I WON'T LEAVE YOU, LOOK WHERE WE ARE. I WRITE ABOUT THESE PLACES, YES, BUT NO SANE GENTLEMAN COMES TO THEM...NOT AT THIS HOUR.
YOU'RE BEING DRAMATIC, CHARLES--AS USUAL. IT WILL ALL WORK OUT SWIMMINGLY.

Obviously words to rue.
TOOK THE WIND OUT OF YOUR SAILS, EH, DICKIE?
WHAT'S GOING ON?! YOUR COLLEAGUES ATTACKED CHARLES AND I...
WELL, OBVIOUSLY YOU'VE BEEN DONE A GOOD'UN-- LOOK AT'CHA, STRUNG UP LIKE A PHEASANT-- N' ME, I COULDN'T BE HAPPIER.
BUT WHY, SIMON? WE'RE FRIENDS! AT LEAST I THOUGHT WE WERE...
FRIENDS WIF YOU?
I HATE YOU. NO, NO, I DESPISE YOU...SWANNING AROUND, DICKIE SWIFT, ALL AIRS N' FANCY WORDS N' NECKTIES.

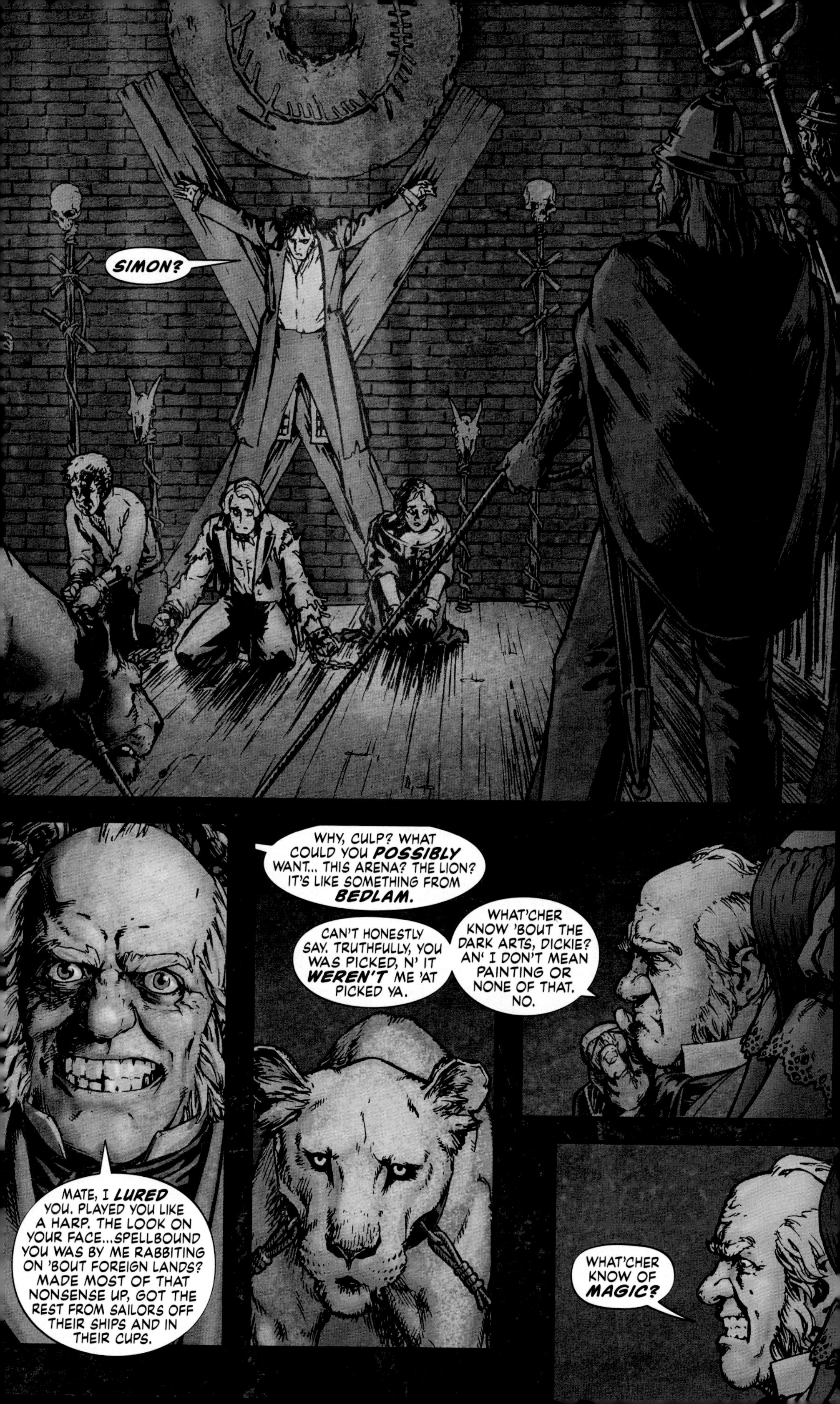

SIMON?

WHY, CULP? WHAT COULD YOU **POSSIBLY** WANT... THIS ARENA? THE LION? IT'S LIKE SOMETHING FROM **BEDLAM.**

CAN'T HONESTLY SAY. TRUTHFULLY, YOU WAS PICKED, N' IT **WEREN'T** ME 'AT PICKED YA.

WHAT'CHER KNOW 'BOUT THE DARK ARTS, DICKIE? AN' I DON'T MEAN PAINTING OR NONE OF THAT. NO.

Y'SEE, I KNOW WHAT I AM.
I WALK THE STREETS. I'VE HAD A LIFETIME CLOSER TO THE DIRT, AND MOST ALL THE WHILE LOOKING AT THE UNDERSIDE OF PEOPLE'S CHINS.
NO.
I CAN'T BE TALL.
BUT I CAN HAVE POWER.
FELL INTO LEARNING ABOUT THE DARK ARTS FROM MY OLD GRANDMUM. WITCH, SHE WAS. GYPSY WITCH.
HARD FOR ME, THOUGH, ON ACCOUNT O' ME NOT ABLE TO READ AND ALL, BUT I'M A PERSISTENT BLOKE, SO I FOUND MY OWN WAYS TO SCHOOL.
FOUND THESE ESTEEMED FOLKS TO SHARE MY HOPE AND INTERESTS. FOUND SPELLS.
FOUND A GODDESS WHO'D GRANT ME MY DREAMS.
RICHARD, ARE YOU LISTENING TO THIS?!
I'M SORRY, CHARLES. I SHOULD HAVE LISTENED TO YOU AND KEPT CLEAR OF HIM.

SPELL I'M ABOUT TO CAST WILL EVOKE--LIKE THAT WORD? EVOKE?--IT'LL SUMMON HER...SCATHACH. "SHE WHO STRIKES FEAR."
OR WILL, ONCE I'M DONE.
SO THIS--THE LION, RICHARD TIED UP THERE--HOW IN YOUR UNHINGED STATE DOES ALL...DOES ANY... COULD ANY OF IT GIVE YOU POWER?
IT COME TO ME IN DREAMS... SOME SLUMBER, N' SOME OF THE PIPE, I CONFESS, BUT ALL OF THEM LIKE I WAS ENTERING A SPECIAL DREAMING PLACE, SO REAL THEY WERE.
THE VOICES TOLD ME THEY NEEDED SACRIFICES... THAT'S THESE OFF'A THE STREET AND YOU, THE NOTED CHARLES DICKENS, FOR GOOD MEASURE.
THEIR MURDER MUST BE FROM A PRIMAL CREATURE. A WILD THING. THOUGHT I MIGHT GO BEAR, BUT I KNEW...IN MY HEART I KNEW A LION'D DO THE TRICK.
AND YOU, DICKIE, YOU WERE REQUEST-ED SPECIAL-LIKE...FROM SCATHACH HERSELF. NOT SURE WHY, BUT YOU'RE NOT JUST ANYONE. NO.
YEAH, FUNNY HOW THAT PLAYED OUT. MET YOU TO GET THE LION, BUT AFTER-WARDS...MY DREAM WHISPERS TOLD ME THE GREAT SCATHACH WANTED YOU.
NOW. THE SPELL.
HE'S INSANE, DICK! MADNESS!
OH, YOU THINK? MAYBE YOU'RE RIGHT... MAYBE THIS IS MAD. STILL...

THAT'S IT! FREE THE BEAST!
THE SPELL NEEDS BLOOD!
...S' BLEEDIN' BEAUTIFUL N' ALL.

RRRRRRR
RAOW!
WAIT! NUHNO... S' NOT SUPPOSED T--
RICHARD?!
RICHARD!!

If I recall the moment I became the Shade—the instant—it is just that, a moment in time.
But simul-taneously in my memory it took years.
Cast adrift on an ebon tide. Agony, bliss, icy numbness, conflagrant light, anger, calm.
And I became someone new.
Fleeting memories of my wife...
...of my sons...
...of my old life were as the memories of another man.
Understand that, while I was feeling and drifting, I had no awareness of my actions in the real world, and to this day no recollection.
Although, as he subsequently related to me, I apparently saved Charles...

Then, like the Richard Swift of old, those memories ebbed to nothing.
I wish my actions had been the same for Culp's wife...
ADELE! ADELE!
...dragging him from the stygian mass and hurling him to where he found purchase away from the dark.
...for she seemed but a witless vassal in his thrall and ill-deserving of her fate

The lion died, too, I'm sorry to say.
But my own "death" was upon me by this time...
For in that moment the blackness overcame me.
And I was oblivion.

I emerged from my idyll with a mind as witless as the late Mrs. Culp.
Scant memory.
The fact that Culp and Charles were gone was one I didn't note or register.
(Survivors both. I'd later learn that Culp was in fact now a creature of shadow like myself.)
(Oh, and it would also be many years before I learned the full truth behind this night. Why did Culp's pagan Goddess of choice, or Culp's flawed spell...or whatever it was...elect me to possess this power over darkness?)
(Scathach would tell me herself, as it happens. Though not for 87 years.)
I left the dead in that fearful arena...

...and walked as if within a dream...
...stumbling into the light...
...and was only half aware of hooves on cobblestones as Piers Ludlow's carriage came upon me.
ARE YOU SOUND, SIR? ARE YOU WELL?
NO, THOUGH I THANK YOU FOR ASKING ME. I AM UNCLEAR.
I FEAR MY MEMORY HAS BEEN TAKEN.
I confess in the now of Opal and my life today, I try as often as I am able to think of my past actions as those of another man.
Richard Swift. Naive, overly trusting, overly concerned with money, too, if I gather my faults honestly.
But I was also a husband and a father...flawed in those departments, too, I'm sure, but at least...at least...what?
What can I say? Truthfully, I thought it best to leave them...to spare them what I had become, but I see now there was nothing gallant about my decision...
...and it was this that perhaps led to the weakness in the character of my bloodline that manifested itself in the present. I am sad, I am guilty.
But...
I know, too, that the future may yet offer me respite... Opal, Hope and tomorrow... if I face that tomorrow with a greater understanding of my weaknesses.
The End

Unused variant cover for issue #8 by Jill Thompson & Trish Mulvihill

The Shade character sketches
by Cully Hamner

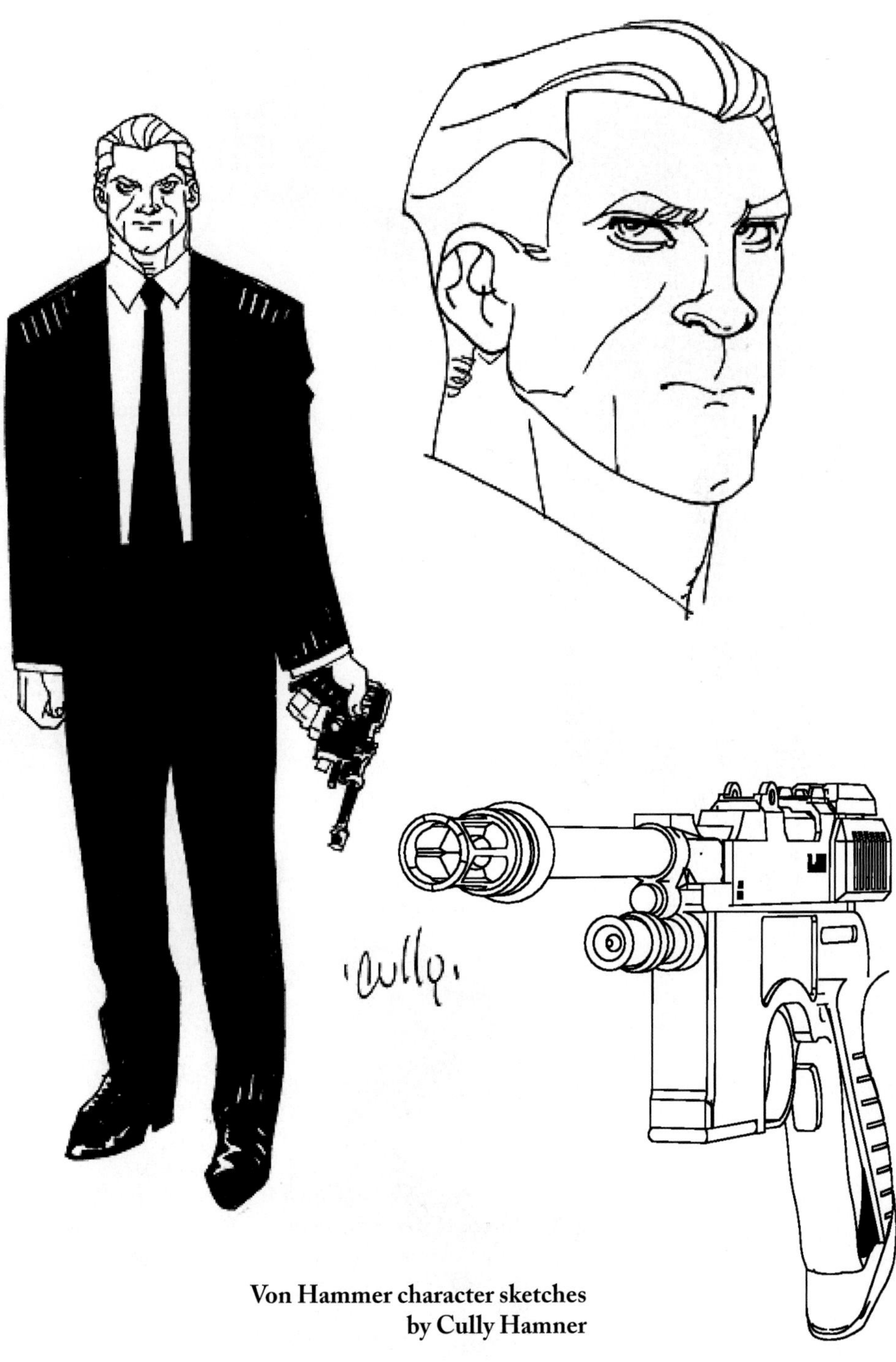

**Von Hammer character sketches
by Cully Hamner**

Les Diaboliques character sketches
by Cully Hamner

Argonaut character sketch
by Cully Hamner

La Sangre character sketches
by Javier Pulido

Inquisitor character sketches
by Javier Pulido

Montpelier character sketches
by Javier Pulido

Celestial Pharaoh character sketch by Frazer Irving

Nhut character sketch by Frazer Irving

Thon character sketch by Frazer Irving

St. Aubrey character sketch by Frazer Irving